STRUCTURED EMPLOYMENT INTERVIEWING

STRUCTURED EMPLOYMENT INTERVIEWING

❖

Paul J. Taylor
and
Michael P. O'Driscoll

Gower

Published by
Gower Publishing Limited
Gower House
Croft Road
Aldershot
Hampshire GU11 3HR
England

Gower
Old Post Road
Brookfield
Vermont 05036
USA

Paul Taylor and Michael O'Driscoll have asserted their right under the
Copyright, Designs and Patents Act 1988 to be identified as the
authors of this work.

British Library Cataloguing in Publication Data

Taylor, Paul J.
Structured Employment Interviewing
I. Title   II. O'Driscoll, Michael P.
658.31124

ISBN 0–566–07589–X

Library of Congress Cataloging-in-Publication Data

Taylor, Paul J.
Structured employment interviewing /
Paul J. Taylor and Michael P. O'Driscoll
p.   cm.
Includes bibliographical references and index.
ISBN 0–566–07589–X
1. Employment interviewing.   I. O'Driscoll, Michael P.
II. Title
HF5549.5.I6T39 1995
858.3'1124–dc20
94–34945
CIP

Typeset in Garamond by Raven Typesetters, Chester, Cheshire
Printed in Great Britain by
Hartnoll's Ltd, Bodmin

CONTENTS

LIST OF FIGURES

PREFACE

❖

Over the past decade, research and descriptive articles about structured employment interviewing have been prominent in the personnel selection literature. Among researchers who have studied them and managers who have used them there is agreement that, compared with unstructured selection interviews, structured interviews predict more accurately who will succeed in the job and are fairer to applicants because interviewers' questions are all job-related.

Managers have always been concerned with accurately predicting job success, but the question of fairness has become increasingly important in the past 25 years. An increased sensitivity has developed to providing individuals with equal employment opportunities regardless of gender, ethnicity or age, and, like other personnel selection methods, the employment interview has attracted its share of criticism. While equal employment opportunity laws vary across countries and even over time within the same country, one of the best means an organization has of establishing fair employment practices is to ensure that any selection tests and interview questions are clearly job-related. In the case of the employment interview, the solution is to make it more structured.

However, despite enthusiasm for the improved validity and fairness of structured interviews, surprisingly little practical guidance is available for those who regularly conduct employment interviews. Brief journal articles and most current textbooks on personnel selection, human resource management and industrial-organizational psychology provide overviews of how structured interviews work, but few references exist that afford enough detail on how to actually implement them. Most large organizations that have used structured employment interviews have done so either by purchasing a training package or by hiring psychologists to develop interview questions.

The purpose of this book is to make available to people who oversee and conduct employment interviews in organizations the practical guidance and tools necessary to use a structured approach. After reviewing the traditional, unstructured interview in Chapter 1, we describe how structured interviews differ in approach and in predictive accuracy (Chapter 2). Chapters 3, 4 and 5 introduce specific procedures for the two most common types of structured interviews (behavioural description and situational interviews), and in Chapter 6 we discuss what is involved in implementing the structured interview approach. Finally, Part II consists of examples of necessary forms, lists of common competencies and sample interview questions, and examples of a few structured interviews.

We have based the book on our experience in teaching managers and other personnel how to conduct structured employment interviews, introducing the approach to many organizations and conducting research on structured interviews. For those interested in reading further about the empirical basis of structured interviews we have tried to balance the book with references to research and other writing as well as practical illustrations and materials for the practitioner.

Most professional disciplines contain some jargon and abbreviations in order to avoid the repeated use of lengthy terms and definitions, and the field of personnel selection is no different. Therefore, in addition to providing definitions the first time we use a technical term or abbreviation, we have included a glossary at the back of this book for easy reference.

Finally, we would like to acknowledge three of our students, Geoff Annals, Winnie Fan and Bruce Small, who have conducted structured interview research and applications, some of which have been used as examples in this book. We also thank two local organizations, Environment Waikato and Health Waikato, for permitting us to include in Part II two structured interviews developed for their organizations.

Paul J. Taylor
Michael P. O'Driscoll

PART I

❖

1

THE TRADITIONAL INTERVIEW APPROACH

❖

Organizations rely heavily on people to achieve their objectives. People fulfil essential roles in the functioning of organizations and, conversely, human performance failures can be extremely costly for organizations. Hence decisions about hiring, placing and developing employees are critical aspects of human resource practice. Studies carried out in Britain, Europe, the United States and other countries have illustrated, in particular, that correct decisions about hiring can have a huge impact on productivity, in terms of monetary gains, as well as quantity and quality of service (see, for example, Dipboye, 1991; Landy, 1989; Smith and George, 1992).

A large variety of personnel selection techniques have been developed over the years, including psychological tests, psychomotor tests, cognitive ability tests, work samples, assessment centres, letters of reference, biographical data, and interviewing. Each of these selection procedures is based on the premise that it can differentiate between applicants who will be successful on the job and those who will be unsuccessful. The effectiveness of these methods has been the subject of intensive research. However, of all the techniques available for hiring new staff, the approach which is most commonly used is the interview.

Interviewing as part of the procedure for selecting employees has a long history in human resource practice. Despite its popularity, however, the selection interview has not had a good track record in choosing suitable job applicants. As we shall discuss a little later, research suggests that the typical employment interview does not yield good hiring decisions.

This inconsistency between research evidence indicating limited effectiveness of the selection interview and its obvious appeal to human

3

resource practitioners and managers alike has led to people asking why the interview approach is so popular. Many reasons have been noted (Arvey and Campion, 1982; Dipboye, 1991). First is a pervasive belief that the interview assesses personal attributes (such as interpersonal skills) which other techniques cannot readily determine. Face-to-face interaction with applicants is believed to be necessary to gauge these types of characteristics. Second, interviewers often feel that they are skilled in ascertaining the skills and characteristics of individuals and that they can make good judgements about applicant suitability from their interactions with that person. Third, interviews are seen as a two-way street. As well as affording employers an opportunity to view job applicants, they also provide an opportunity for applicants to obtain information about the organization and their prospective employer. Finally, it is clear that managers and employers like interviewing and enjoy the opportunity to meet job applicants in person. It would seem that interviewing may serve a variety of needs, not all of which are directly associated with the actual selection decision.

In this book we shall be presenting methods for conducting employment interviews so that valid selection decisions can be achieved. More particularly, we shall concentrate attention on structured approaches to interviewing, which have been found to be considerably more reliable and valid than traditional interview methods. Before discussing the structured approach, however, we shall examine how interviews are typically carried out, and some of the problems and limitations of the selection interview as it is commonly utilized.

HOW SELECTION INTERVIEWS ARE TYPICALLY CONDUCTED

Traditionally, employment interviews have been carried out in an unstructured manner. Some attention may be given to interview length and, where there are several interviewers, there may be some discussion prior to the interview about the nature of questions to be asked (based on the applicant's résumé or letter of application). However, standardized questions are not drawn up before the interview commences, nor is there any standard format for the interview process itself, which is left very much up to the judgement of the interviewer. In fact, in many cases different applicants are asked quite different sets of questions, and the direction of questioning is determined predominantly by interviewers' personal preferences and information supplied by candidates in their job application, rather than by questions which focus on predetermined job-related issues. Most interviews lack standardized questions and systematic procedures for evaluating applicants (Dipboye, 1991).

Traditional selection interviews often deal with personal attributes of the applicant, such as 'personality', physical characteristics and non-verbal behaviours (Daniel and Valencia, 1991). One illustration of this is provided by Gatewood and Feild (1990), who describe the attention often given to the body language of interviewees. As an illustration, Gatewood and Feild have noted the recommendation of one author that interviewers should examine the hand movements of the applicant during the course of the interview. Raising the fingers of both hands and joining them together to form a steeple is a gesture which supposedly indicates that the applicant feels 'superior'. According to the author, this non-verbal behaviour suggests that the applicant is undesirable for appointment. Similarly, folding one's arms across the chest can be interpreted by interviewers as being closed or 'standoffish', when in fact it may simply indicate that the candidate is nervous. As Gatewood and Feild comment, many such recommendations are made on the basis of little or no empirical evidence.

Many other problems have also been noted in the traditional approach to selection interviewing. As early as 1964, Mayfield summarized research findings which suggested that unstructured interviews suffer from the following deficiencies:

○   Information is not covered consistently across interviews.
○   Different interviewers give different importance weightings to the same information.
○   Interviewers often make their decision about an applicant very early on in the interview, often within the first four to five minutes; the remaining time is then spent looking for information which would confirm early impressions.
○   Because their primary task is often to eliminate 'unsuitable' candidates, interviewers are frequently influenced more by unfavourable (or negative) information about applicants than they are by favourable (positive) information.
○   Interviewers often spend more time during the interview talking rather than listening to the applicant.

Similar issues have been highlighted by Schmitt (1976), who noted, in addition, that research indicates that early impressions have more impact on interviewer judgements than later information, and non-verbal cues (such as eye- and hand-movements) are given more attention than information provided verbally by the candidate. Furthermore, similarity between the interviewer and applicant in gender, race and other physical characteristics may have a marked influence on selection interview decisions (Dipboye, 1991).

Other biases which are frequently evident in selection interviews are halo effects, differences between interviewers in leniency versus stringency, and contrast effects. Halo effects occur when one personal attribute, judged as either positive or negative, is presumed to reflect the whole 'personality' of the individual. For instance, a person who is perceived as physically attractive will frequently be considered more intelligent, sociable, and caring, even in the absence of information about these attributes (Deaux and Wrightsman, 1988). Clearly, such generalizations can produce distortions in interviewer evaluations of an individual's potential for success on the job.

Leniency/stringency refers to differences between interviewers in their approach to making interview judgements. Some interviewers take a very hard line, looking for negative qualities that might discount a job applicant, whereas other interviewers focus on the positive attributes of individuals. These differences can lead to marked discrepancies between interviewers in their judgements of the same candidates.

Finally, given that interviewers are usually considering more than one applicant for a position, contrast effects can emerge when the characteristics of one candidate are compared with those of individuals who have already been interviewed, rather than against some previously determined behavioural criterion. This comparison may lead to either overevaluation or underevaluation of the capabilities of a particular applicant, depending on where he or she falls in the order of interviews. For instance, Wexley and his colleagues found that, while judgements about candidates who were either very highly or very poorly qualified for a sales position were not overly influenced by contrast effects, ratings of applicants whose qualifications were 'average' were significantly affected by whether the previous applicants were high or low in suitability for the position (Wexley, Yukl, Kovacs and Sanders, 1972).

It is mainly because of the above biases and limitations that the traditional unstructured interview has been found to have rather poor predictive accuracy. The accuracy of any approach to selecting staff, including different interview approaches, is referred to as its *validity*. To illustrate the validity of unstructured interviews, as well as the validity of structured interviews and other selection methods discussed later in the book, we need to first explain how the validity of a personnel selection method is determined and numerically represented.

VALIDITY

The validity of a selection method is usually determined by correlating scores on the predictor variable (interviewer judgement, in the case of the selection interview) with measures of the relevant criterion, which is typically job performance. Because studies of this type involve an assessment of the relationship between scores on the selection method with a criterion, they are referred to as criterion-related validation studies.

Predictor and criterion scores can be collected at either two points in time or at the same time. When collected at different times, the predictor data are gathered when candidates apply and the criterion data are noted after they have been on the job long enough for job performance data, such as performance appraisal ratings or objective indices, to exist. In other cases, however, predictive and criterion data are collected concurrently, using existing job incumbents.

The relationship between predictor and criterion scores is represented statistically as a validity coefficient, ranging from zero (where the ordering of applicants on the selection method bears no relationship at all with their ordering in terms of actual job performance), to 1.00 (where there is a perfect one-to-one relationship between applicants' predictor and job performance scores).

RELIABILITY

The reliability of a personnel selection method refers to its *consistency* (for example, consistency of interview judgements over time or between interviewers). Reliability is a necessary, but not sufficient requirement for validity. In other words, a selection method must yield generally consistent judgements about candidates in order to be accurate. However, those judgements could be consistently wrong. In the case of the traditional selection interview, judgements have usually been found to be inconsistent between interviewers and, even when consistent, they do not predict future job performance very well.

RESEARCH ON RELIABILITY AND VALIDITY

Several studies have been conducted on the reliability and validity of unstructured interviews. In an early piece of research, Wagner (1949) obtained an average correlation of 0.37 between interviewer judgements and future job performance. More recently, Janz (1982) found a correlation of just 0.07 between standard interview judgements about applicants and their performance ratings, while Reilly and Chao (1982) and Hunter and Hunter (1984) reported coefficients of 0.19 and 0.14 respectively. From a meta-analysis of research in this area, Wiesner and Cronshaw (1988) observed validity coefficients which ranged between 0.20 and 0.37 for this kind of interview. In short, support for the predictive validity of unstructured interviewing is not impressive.

There is also little evidence of consistency in interviewer judgements. Wiesner and Cronshaw (1988), for instance, found an average reliability for unstructured interviews of just 0.61, which reflects relatively low agreement between interviewers in their judgements about job applicants. This lack of agreement can be attributed to many of the factors outlined above, and highlights the persistent difficulties encountered with unstructured selection interviewing. On a more optimistic note, Wiesner and Cronshaw's analyses, along with research conducted by other investigators, has obtained more promising results for structured interview approaches, which we shall describe in detail in the following chapters.

HOW TO IMPROVE SELECTION INTERVIEWING

While the typical interviewing procedure clearly falls short as a procedure for hiring new staff, there are ways of enhancing the quality of the interview and making it a valuable tool for selection purposes. Fundamentally, as we shall discuss in the following chapters, this entails making the interview more 'structured'. By this we mean that questions which are asked of job applicants are related to the job, the same questions are asked of all candidates, and their responses are evaluated using systematic 'scoring' procedures (rather than *ad hoc* subjective evaluations).

One important way to improve the reliability and validity of the selection interviewing is to ask applicants questions which are specific and relevant to the job. As noted earlier, interviewers frequently focus on information which is not of direct relevance to future job performance (such as family matters, hobbies and interests). Concentrating on job knowledge and skills related to job performance increases the ability of interviewers to estimate applicants' likelihood of success in the job (Gatewood and Feild, 1990). As we mention later, basing interview questions on a systematic analysis of the job will ensure that questions are relevant. In Chapters 3–5 we describe procedures for developing specific job-related questions.

Exploring the same issues with all job applicants is another important aspect of selection interviewing. Where interviewers vary the nature of questions asked of different candidates, it is likely that they will be making judgements on the basis of different kinds of information. For example, there is evidence to suggest that female and male applicants may be asked different questions during an employment interview (Berry and Houston, 1993). Females are more likely than males to be questioned about their spouse and children and how they will manage family matters if they were appointed. Not only do such questions discriminate unfairly between applicants, but they also lead to hiring decisions which are based upon irrelevant details. Valid comparisons between candidates can only be made when the same kinds of information are sought from all applicants.

Finally, traditional, unstructured interviews typically do not use a systematic approach for evaluating applicants' responses to interview questions. Under these circumstances, judgements about the quality of one person's responses may be based on different criteria from the responses given by another person. The perceptual biases discussed earlier may come into play, influencing how interviewers react toward different candidates. An applicant who is perceived to be similar to the interviewers themselves can be evaluated more favourably than one who is seen as 'different', even when both applicants provide the same answers to questions. Furthermore, interviewers will vary among themselves in terms of how they gauge applicants' responses. Again the end result will be a less than optimal hiring decision.

Another point which warrants mention in this context is training for interviewers. Often, little or no training in interview technique is provided for people engaged in employment interviewing. In some cases there may be a brief meeting of the interview panel before the interviews are conducted, but little effort is made to 'coach' individuals in the art and science of effective interviewing. Structured approaches to selection interviewing, on the other hand, necessitate considerable development of interviewing skills and therefore require careful preparation of interviewers. While this can be time-consuming, it also ensures that the actual interview process itself will be conducted more rigorously and systematically, and consequently that better decisions will be reached.

All of the above issues are addressed by the structured approaches to selection interviewing which we outline in the following chapters. Developing questions which are specific and job-related, asking the same questions of all candidates, and constructing a systematic method for evaluating applicant responses will enable interviewers to avoid the problems discussed in this chapter and will enhance the reliability and validity of the interview process.

References

Arvey, R.D. and Campion, J.E. (1982), 'The Employment Interview: A Summary and Review of Recent Research', *Personnel Psychology*, **35**, 281–322.

Berry, L.M. and Houston, J.P. (1993), *Psychology at Work*. Madison, WI: Brown & Benchmark.

Daniel, C. and Valencia, S. (1991), 'Structured Interviewing Simplified',

Public Personnel Management, **20** (2), 127–34.

Deaux, K. and Wrightsman, L. (1988), *Social Psychology,* (5th edn). Pacific Grove, CA: Brooks/Cole.

Dipboye, R.L. (1991), *Selection Interviews: Process Perspectives.* Cincinnati, OH: South-Western.

Gatewood, R.D. and Feild, H.S. (1990), *Human Resource Selection,* (2nd edn). Chicago: Dryden Press.

Hunter, J.E. and Hunter, R.F. (1984), 'Validity and Utility of Alternative Predictors of Job Performance'. *Psychological Bulletin,* **96**, 72–98.

Janz, T. (1982), 'Initial Comparisons of Patterned Behavior Description Interviews Versus Unstructured Interviews', *Journal of Applied Psychology,* **67**, 577–80.

Landy, F.J. (1989), *Psychology of Work Behavior,* (4th edn). Pacific Grove, CA: Brooks/Cole.

Reilly, R.A. and Chao, G.T. (1982), 'Validity and Fairness of Some Alternative Selection Procedures', *Personnel Psychology,* **35**, 1–61.

Schmitt, N. (1976), 'Social and Situational Determinants of Interview Decisions: Implications for the Employment Interview', *Personnel Psychology,* **29**, 79–101.

Smith, M.C. and George, D.I. (1992), 'Selection Methods', in C.L. Cooper and I.T. Robertson (eds), *International Review of Industrial and Organizational Psychology,* **7**, 55–97.

Wagner, R. (1949), 'The Employment Interview: A Critical Summary', *Personnel Psychology,* **2**, 17–46.

Wexley, K.N., Yukl, G.A., Kovacs, S.Z. and Sanders, R.E. (1972), 'Importance of Contrast Effects in Employment Interviews', *Journal of Applied Psychology,* **56**, 45–48.

Weisner, W.H. and Cronshaw, S.F. (1988), 'A Meta-Analytic Investigation of the Impact of Interview Format and Degree of Structure on the Validity of the Employment Interview', *Journal of Occupational Psychology,* **62**, 577–80.

2

THE STRUCTURED INTERVIEW APPROACH

❖

The roots of structured approaches to selection interviews go back about 30 years, when a few researchers suggested that interviews could be improved by basing questions on thorough job analyses, including examining critical incidents which have occurred on the job. Some researchers published reports on conducting employment interviews in more structured ways, and provided evidence of the superiority of these interviews over traditional, unstructured interviews. In the early 1980s, specific structured interview procedures were introduced, along with research reports of their validity and, since that time, hundreds of studies and articles have been published on employment interviewing.

THE PREDICTIVE ACCURACY OF STRUCTURED VERSUS UNSTRUCTURED INTERVIEWS

The primary purpose of the interview is to predict which of a group of job candidates is likely to succeed best in the job. In order to compare the accuracy of the structured employment interview to the unstructured interview, we need to first review how the accuracy of selection methods is assessed and represented.

There have been nearly 200 studies which have assessed the validity of different types of interviews and a handful of reviews of such studies. The most comprehensive review of validation studies concerning structured versus unstructured interviews was conducted by Wiesner and Cronshaw (1988). As with most other reviews, they statistically combined studies to

11

estimate the average validities of structured and unstructured interviews. Based on the 152 studies they analysed, covering results from over 50,000 interviews, they estimated the average validity of the structured interview to be 0.62. Other reviews of validation studies on structured and unstructured interviews have also found significant differences in validity.

Improving the validity of an organization's selection system through the use of structured interviews can result in substantial increases in productivity and cost savings. For example, Harman Management, the largest franchisee of Kentucky Fried Chicken in the USA, has estimated that it has achieved a $9,500,000 increase in sales volume and $1,240,000 cost savings in reduced staff turnover through using structured interviews. Brewers Joshua Tetley, in England, have noted significant increases in profits over a five-year period as a result of selecting top performing managers through structured interviews (Lunn, 1993). The J.C. Penny Company, a large retail chain in the United States, estimates that it has received a $10 million payoff over two and a half years by adopting a structured interview approach (Cascio, 1992).

One practical consideration related to validity is the cost-effectiveness of selection processes. Again structured interviews rate highly in comparison with other techniques. Structured interviews are less 'expensive' to implement than work samples and assessment centres, which also have high selection validities. Structured interviews are less complex to develop and less time-consuming and expensive to conduct than these alternative approaches. Certainly they are more costly than conventional unstructured interviews, but the gains in validity far outweigh the costs of implementation.

FAIRNESS OF STRUCTURED VERSUS UNSTRUCTURED INTERVIEWS

Organizations worldwide have become increasingly concerned that their personnel selection procedures do not discriminate against individuals in terms of gender, ethnicity, age and physical disabilities. Many countries now have legislation requiring the provision of equal employment opportunities (EEO) in personnel selection practices. As discussed in Chapter 1, the unstructured interview is susceptible to interviewer bias in that questions which are not job-related are frequently asked, different job candidates are often asked different questions, and the basis on which interview decisions are made typically lacks clarity and documentation.

There are differences in EEO legislation across countries, and legislation often changes within individual countries, but two principles offer a strong defence against interview bias: make all interview questions job-related; systematically analyse candidates' responses. Before proceeding to a discussion of specific approaches to structured interviews, we shall spend a little time examining these two general principles. Structured interviews are based on these two principles, and therefore have been viewed as more fair than unstructured interviews.

The legality of selection procedures has come under close scrutiny in recent years because of concerns over the fairness of personnel selection methods (Gabris and Rock, 1991). In the United States, for example, there have been several challenges to the use of psychological tests, especially personality tests, for hiring new staff. As a result of these concerns, employers are now looking more closely at the legal standing of the methods they adopt to select personnel. Because of their concentration on specific job-related behaviours, their standardized procedures – which ensure that minorities and other groups are not unfairly discriminated against – and the documentation they provide about how hiring decisions have been made, structured interviews avoid many of the pitfalls of other selection methods such as personality testing and unstructured interviews. Latham (1989) has reported data which suggest that structured interviews are also perceived by representatives of the legal profession as more legally defensible than unstructured interviews.

TYPES OF STRUCTURED INTERVIEWS

Variations in the way to conduct structured interviews have emerged over recent years, but the two most prominent approaches are the behavioural description interview (BDI, also known as *patterned* behavioural description interviews, or PBDIs) and the situational interview. While there are important distinctions between these two interview types, they share three common elements: interview questions are based on a thorough job analysis; job candidates are asked the same (or very similar) questions; candidates' answers are rated systematically. In this chapter, we shall look first at similarities between these two types of structured interviews, and then at their differences before going on to a more in-depth description of each technique in the following two chapters.

INTERVIEW QUESTIONS ARE BASED ON A THOROUGH JOB ANALYSIS

In a structured interview, *all* questions are job-related, and stem from a job analysis. A job analysis is a systematic process of collecting job-related information. Through this technique, the core competencies required for successful performance are specified, so that interview questions can be developed to assess candidates on each of those competencies.

One of the hallmarks of job analysis is the collection of job-related information from various sources, such as managers, incumbents and others familiar with the target position. In contrast, preparation for an unstructured interview often involves only the position manager and a personnel specialist, who review general job descriptions and plan a few broad questions.

Using a number of sources of job analysis information helps avoid any idiosyncratic biases of a single person. These biases can lead to the inclusion of a selection criterion which is unrelated to job success, to missing an important competency or placing too much or too little emphasis on particular requirements.

Consider a manager hiring a replacement for an assistant who has taken another job after only one year in his/her present position. The manager decides that one of the most important requirements for the job is that the new person intends to stay in the position for quite some time. While stability may be important for this position, the manager may be placing too much emphasis on this single attribute, losing sight of other important selection criteria. A job analysis which includes input from a number of people involved with the job is likely to place the importance of the 'stability' criterion in perspective.

JOB CANDIDATES ARE ASKED THE SAME (OR VERY SIMILAR) QUESTIONS

Many interviewers who use an unstructured approach place emphasis on the building of rapport in the interview and do so, in part, by making the interview an informal conversation. Different questions are asked of different candidates because each informal conversation takes its own course. One concern with this approach is that asking different questions of different candidates implies that all questions are probably not job-related. Given that candidates are applying for the same job, keeping questions job-related means that all candidates will be asked similar questions.

Another concern with an informal interview approach which allows differences in questions across candidates is the difficulty of evaluating candidates' suitability for the position. Comparing two candidates who have been asked different questions is like comparing apples and oranges. Candidate 1 should not be credited for experience shared in the interview if Candidate 2 was not asked about similar experiences.

The emphasis, in structured interviews, on asking a similar set of questions of all candidates does not mean that building rapport is unimportant. As with unstructured interviews, structured interviews must leave candidates with a favourable impression of the organization and the interview. This is important to increase the likelihood that the best-performing job candidate accepts the offer, and to ensure that the image of the organization is maintained or enhanced in the eyes of candidates who are not offered a position. However, building rapport is not seen as the most important objective of the interview.

JOB CANDIDATES' ANSWERS ARE RATED SYSTEMATICALLY

Successful performance on most jobs typically requires the incumbent to be competent in more than one area. In structured interviews, each of these competencies is usually judged individually in order to prevent interviewers' judgement of one aspect of a candidate carrying too much weight in the selection decisions. This is referred to as a 'halo effect' (*see* Chapter 1). For example, an interviewer who only makes a global judgement about the employability of a job candidate could overrate a very articulate job candidate despite the fact that this candidate is weak in other core areas. In structured interviews, the relative weight of different competencies is often determined *before* interviews are conducted, to help avoid halo error.

When more than one interviewer is used, which is often the case in structured interviews, the ratings of all interviewers are combined systematically to prevent one interviewer's judgement carrying too much weight. Interviewers rate candidates' performance in the structured interview individually, before ratings are combined to arrive at a final score for each applicant.

DIFFERENCES BETWEEN BDIs AND SITUATIONAL INTERVIEWS

The major difference between behavioural description and situational interviews is the type of questions asked of job candidates. The BDI includes questions about specific *past* situations candidates have faced and how they have responded to them (that is 'behavioural descriptions), while the situational interview uses questions about what applicants *would* do if faced with specific *hypothetical* situations. Applicants for a customer service position in a department store might be asked in a BDI to recall a situation in which they had to deal with a very angry customer. Candidates would be asked to describe the situation, what they actually did, and the outcome of the situation. Conversely, candidates in a situational interview might be asked to describe how they *would* deal with an angry customer (who is returning a defective item to the department store for the second time).

To many experienced interviewers, asking job candidates about their past experience and about how they would handle hypothetical job situations seems very much like what they already do in interviews, but BDI and situational interview questions are quite different from those commonly asked in traditional employment interviews. In BDIs, job candidates are asked to describe very specific situations that are relevant to the target position, along with their specific response to the situation and the outcome of that response. In traditional, unstructured interviews, most interviewers ask many questions regarding candidates' past experiences, but they are usually about the applicant's *general experience*, not about specific situations faced (Janz, 1989).

Similarly, unstructured interviewers often ask a few hypothetical '*what would you do if...*' questions, which look much like the questions asked in situational interviews. However, the hypothetical questions used in situational interviews are carefully developed to represent key job requirements and the predetermined scoring key minimizes the effect of interviewer bias on the evaluation of candidates' answers.

To see how a lack of a scoring key permits interviewer bias in judging answers, consider a sales manager interviewing candidates for a sales position. The sales manager asks a candidate to pretend to sell him something, such as a pen. After the interview, the manager decides how effective the applicant was in the simulated sale. Without a predetermined scoring key, the sales manager is prone to contaminating his/her judgement about the effectiveness of the candidate's presentation by the common interview biases discussed in Chapter 1 (for example, first impressions).

There are a few other minor differences between BDI and situational interviews. Scoring keys, which provide interviewers with specific guidelines for rating particular candidate responses, are always provided in situational interviews and are not often used in BDIs. Also, candidates in a BDI are rated on performance competencies, such as 'customer service orientation' in the previous example, based on the quality and quantity of the descriptions they provide, while candidates in a situational interview are sometimes scored on their answer to *each question.*

Both of these approaches to structured interviewing have proved significantly more valid than unstructured approaches, but one may be more appropriate than the other in particular situations. Of the two, the BDI is more widely used, for it does not require an answer scoring key as in the situational interview, and thus it is easier to develop and it can be used for jobs that have had few or even no previous incumbents. In sum, the BDI approach is most appropriate when many applicants are likely to have related work experience, and when hiring for a position held by only one or a few people in the organization or hiring for a newly created position.

On the other hand, once it has been developed, the situational interview is easier to use because answers can be scored quickly. Managers and personnel staff who conduct situational interviews require less training than those who use BDIs, because they do not need to develop new questions. Because of its greater development costs, the situational interview is best suited for positions for which many people are employed in an organization.

Furthermore, a recent study comparing BDI and situational interview approaches found the latter to have slightly higher validity (Searcy, et al., 1993). This study was unable to determine why situational interviews may have higher validity than BDIs, but the predetermined scoring key of the situational interview is a likely explanation. Such a scoring key probably increases validity through improved between-interviewer reliability. The scoring key used in the situational interview might also be applied to the BDI to improve reliability and validity, as discussed later in Chapter 6.

If you are in a relatively small organization (say, less than 200 staff) in which no single job has more than a few positions, the situational interview is unlikely to be a cost-effective alternative. If you are a member of a larger organization, there is likely to be a place for both BDIs and situational interviews.

The procedures for conducting BDIs and situational interviews are covered in the next three chapters. Since BDIs can be used in more hiring situations than situational interviews, methods for BDIs are described first. We deal with BDIs in two chapters, the first describing how to *prepare* the BDI (Chapter 3), the second on how to *conduct* the BDI (Chapter 4).

Even if your primary interest is in the situational interview, we recommend that you read Chapters 3 and 4 first. Much of how the situational interview is developed, conducted and scored is similar to the BDI, and so in Chapter 5 (situational interviews), we frequently refer back to techniques developed in Chapters 3 and 4.

References

Cascio, W.F. (1992), *Managing Human Resources*, (3rd edn). New York: McGraw Hill.

Gabris, G.T. and Rock, S.M. (1991), 'Situational Interviews and Job-Performance: The Results in One Public Agency', *Public Personnel Management*, **20** (4), 469–83.

Janz, T. (1989), 'The Patterned Behavior Description Interview: The Best Prophet of the Future is the Past', in R.W. Eder and G.R. Ferris (eds), *The*

Employment Interview, 158–68, Newbury Park, CA: Sage.

Latham, G.P. (1989), 'The Reliability, Validity and Practicality of the Situational Interview', in R.W. Eder and G.R. Ferris (eds), *The Employment Interview,* 169–82, Newbury Park, CA: Sage.

Lunn, T. (1993), 'Developing the Talent-Led Company', *Management Development Review,* **6** (3), 21–23.

Searcy, C.A., Woods, P.N., Gatewood, R. and Lance, C. (1993), 'The Validity of Structured Interviews: A Meta-Analytical Search for Moderators'. Paper presented at the Society of Industrial Psychologists 1993 Annual Meeting, San Francisco, CA.

Wiesner, W.H. and Cronshaw, S.F. (1988), 'A Meta-Analytic Investigation of the Impact of Interview Format and Degree of Structure on the Validity of the Employment Interview', *Journal of Occupational Psychology,* **61**, 275–90.

3

PREPARING FOR THE BEHAVIOURAL DESCRIPTION INTERVIEW

❖

The behavioural description interview (BDI) has been traced back to the work of industrial and organizational psychologists in the 1960s, but credit for its development rests largely with Tom Janz, who first published a research report in 1982 on his use of the technique (Janz, 1982).

The underlying principle of BDIs is an old adage of industrial and organizational psychology, referred to as the behavioural consistency principle, that 'past behaviour is the best predictor of future behaviour'. In terms of a hiring situation, it implies that our best guess about what people would do on the job (if hired) is what they have done previously. The BDI provides a framework for determining how applicants have behaved in situations which are similar to those they would experience in the job for which they are applying.

Developing a BDI involves first conducting a job analysis, through which performance competencies (sometimes referred to as performance dimensions) are identified. Next, interview questions are developed which seek behavioural descriptions from job candidates for each competency. Behavioural descriptions are stories of actual situations applicants faced, how they responded (that is, their *behaviour*), and the outcome to the situation. During the interview, candidates are asked both pre-prepared and follow-up questions to ensure that candidates provide complete behavioural descriptions, and the interviewer takes notes of these during the interview for later rating. Finally, candidates are rated on the quality and quantity of relevant behavioural descriptions, and a final selection decision is made. Steps for developing a BDI are presented in Figure 3.1 and are described below.

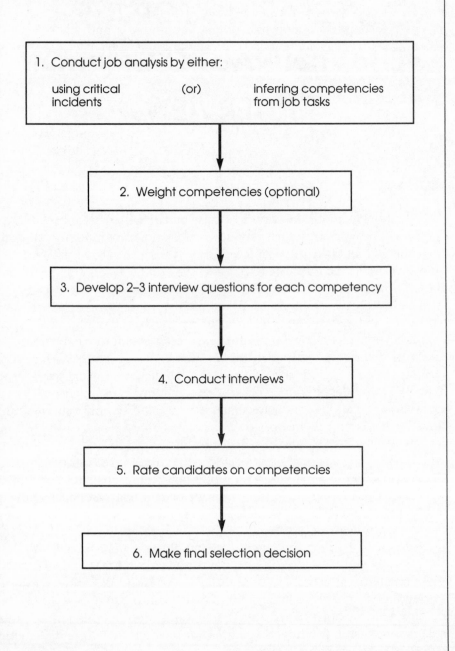

FIGURE 3.1 STEPS FOR DEVELOPING A BEHAVIOURAL DESCRIPTION INTERVIEW

CONDUCTING A JOB ANALYSIS

As with any other method for selecting staff, a BDI should be based on a thorough job analysis. A job analysis is a systematic means of collecting job-related information, and can be used for a variety of purposes, including staff selection, training, performance appraisals and job redesign. When used for staff selection, the critical output of a job analysis is a specification of the knowledge, skills, abilities or other attributes (KSAOs) required to successfully perform the job. Clusters of similar KSAOs are often referred to as 'competencies', or performance 'dimensions'. We refer to them here as competencies, or competency requirements.

Conducting a job analysis to determine competency requirements helps concentrate the interview on the most critical aspects of candidates' past experience. It also allows for a consistent pattern of questions, provides a common basis for the evaluation of all candidates, and minimizes the halo effect in the evaluation of candidates.

One of the hallmarks of job analysis is that several people who are familiar with the job are consulted, which reduces any idiosyncratic perceptions of jobs by particular individuals. When individuals define the competencies required for a job, they very naturally base their judgement on past experiences with people in those jobs. Some of those competencies are likely to be job-related, but some are likely to be unique to an individual incumbent who was either successful or unsuccessful. For example, a sales manager faced with replacing a particularly effective sales person may place inappropriately high value on the candidates having a technical qualification (such as a particular university degree) because the past successful candidate had one. Involving others in the job analysis (in addition to the sales manager) might show that, while a technical degree is an advantage, it is not as important for successful performance as the sales manager had assumed.

There are two approaches for conducting BDI job analysis: the critical incident technique and inferring competency requirements from a task analysis. Of these two, the most thorough approach is the critical incident technique.

THE CRITICAL INCIDENT TECHNIQUE

This technique of job analysis was first developed by Flanagan (1954). Subject-matter experts (SMEs), including supervisors, incumbents, and any others who are knowledgeable about the position, identify particularly effective and ineffective examples of actual past job performance, based on their experience of past and present incumbents of the position.

The incidents are provided as brief stories, without naming particular people involved, and must include the *situation* the incumbent faced, the incumbent's *behaviour*, and the *outcome* of that behaviour. Critical incidents can be obtained either through interviews or questionnaires and, in the case of interviews, either with individuals or with small groups, usually involving three to six SMEs.

Critical incidents must be specific and have actually happened. For example, 'abrasive to co-workers when asked to help' is too general. The following critical incident is at the appropriate level of specificity:

> The incumbent was approached by a co-worker to help retrieve a lost data file, a task which is not within the incumbent's regular duties. The incumbent responded by saying that the co-worker should have maintained a backup file, that it 'served her right', and that retrieving others' lost data files was not part of his responsibility. The co-worker was unable to finish her report by the end of the day, when it was due, and did not approach the incumbent for help again.

Note that this example includes the situation faced by the incumbent (being approached by a co-worker to help retrieve a lost data file ...), the incumbent's behaviour (saying that a backup file should have been maintained...) and the outcome (co-worker was unable to finish the report ...).

In addition to critical incidents of *ineffective* performance, critical incidents of *effective* performance are also included, as in the following example:

Situation   While changing the oil of the customer's car,

Behaviour   the auto mechanic noticed that a brake fluid pipe had severely rusted. He warned the customer of the danger and suggested that it be replaced immediately.

Outcome   The customer thanked the mechanic for noticing the dangerous situation and the garage benefited from the additional business.

When seeking critical incidents from SMEs, start by explaining what a critical incident is (using an actual example or two of past effective or ineffective performance). Sufficient experience is required to provide useful critical incidents, so as a rule of thumb, only seek critical incidents from supervisors or incumbents with at least six months' experience managing, or working in, the target position.

Individual interviews are typically used when the number of SMEs available is small. Small group interviews or questionnaires are used when more individuals are available. Part II A contains a sample form which may be used for critical incident questionnaires or interviews. Ask for as many critical incidents as can be remembered by each SME, which is usually between five and twenty per person, and aim for a total of at least 100 critical incidents for a particular position. In our experience, a small group is likely to generate more critical incidents than one individual, but less than the number that would have been generated if each group member were interviewed alone. Therefore, use small group interviews only when many (for example, 10 or more) individuals will be asked for critical incidents.

Questionnaires can be used instead of, or in addition to, group interviews when there are many SMEs, with the advantage of taking less time to administer. However, there are some limitations to the questionnaire approach. Response rates vary, and while some are returned with many specific critical incidents, others come back with only one or two vague statements (such as, 'Important to get to work on time'). Unlike the interview, the questionnaire provides little opportunity to follow up with SMEs on incomplete details of critical incidents or to obtain additional ones.

Critical incidents can be generated by SMEs thinking of the job as a whole, or thinking of particular aspects of the job, such as the key job tasks or responsibilities. However, by asking SMEs for critical incidents relating to specific aspects of the job, critical incidents relevant to all job aspects are less likely to be included. On the other hand, developing critical incidents from individual tasks runs the risk of omitting those which SMEs associate with the job as a whole but not with any one particular aspect. Consequently, our preference is to seek critical incidents from SMEs for the job as a whole first, and then to follow up by focusing SMEs on specific aspects of the job for which no (or few) critical incidents have been described.

Once generated, the critical incidents are grouped into approximately five to ten competencies by SMEs. Start by looking through the list of critical incidents for patterns of effective/ineffective behaviours. Once the first competency is identified, all critical incidents associated with it are labelled as belonging to that competency, and the remaining critical incidents are searched for the next major competency. This process is reiterated until virtually all critical incidents are accounted for by competencies.

When grouping critical incidents, it is usually helpful to use an existing list of competencies for the job (for example, 'person requirements', 'dimensions'). It may also be helpful to review the list of common competencies which are presented in Part II B, but note that this list is by no means exhaustive. It may be helpful to print critical incidents on index cards which can be grouped in a few different ways before a final categorization is decided.

Generally, the greater the complexity of a job, the greater the number of competencies required. Some critical incidents often fit into more than one competency area, and a few critical incidents do not group into any competency. As a rule of thumb, each competency should consist of at least three or four critical incidents, so isolated critical incidents are typically removed from further analysis.

After a list of competencies has been developed, redundant critical incidents in each competency are removed. Each competency is described with a brief paragraph, and a few of the most representative critical incidents are listed with the definition. (*See* Part II C for an illustration of a final list of job competencies and key critical incidents pertaining to each competency.)

INFERRING COMPETENCY REQUIREMENTS FROM JOB TASKS

The critical incident technique is the most preferable means of job analysis for the BDI because interview questions can be linked directly to past examples of effective and ineffective performance. However, collecting critical incidents in some situations is not feasible. There may have been only one position in the organization, the job may be newly developed, or the job may have been substantially changed. In these instances, there is unlikely to be sufficient critical incidents for all aspects of the job, and competencies should be inferred directly from the tasks.

To infer competencies from tasks, the end results of the job (often referred to as key result areas), accountabilities, accomplishments or job outputs, must be identified. Each end result is broken down into its component tasks, and finally competencies required for those tasks are identified. Thus a person with certain competencies should be able to successfully perform job tasks, which should lead to the attainment of end results, as indicated in Figure 3.2, which is based on the job of store manager for a fast food chain.

SMEs can be asked to list tasks for a particular job, or more commonly, are asked to amend a task list developed by the job analyst using job descriptions, training manuals, or other reference materials, such as the *Dictionary of Occupational Titles* (US Department of Labor, Employment and Training Administration, 1977). SMEs are often asked to rate the importance of each task, and perhaps also its frequency, so that competency requirements associated with the most central tasks can be weighted accordingly.

A sample form for listing and rating tasks is in Part II D, which could be

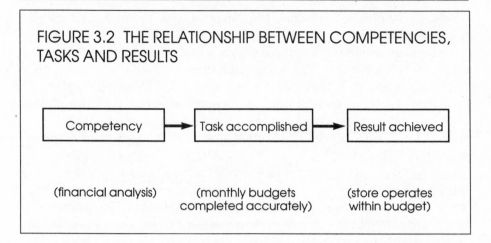

FIGURE 3.2 THE RELATIONSHIP BETWEEN COMPETENCIES, TASKS AND RESULTS

used for either interviews with, or a survey of, SMEs. If interviews are used, they can be conducted either individually or in small groups.

After tasks have been listed and rated, competencies required for successfully completing each task are identified by SMEs. (*See* Part II E for a sample form.) A final list of competencies is developed by removing redundant competencies and those of low importance, such as those associated only with tasks which are accomplished infrequently and those that can be easily trained on the job.

In some situations, competency requirements must be identified for the future, when either the job is expected to change in some way, or those hired for the position are also being selected for their potential to perform future jobs to which they are likely to be promoted. In both cases, SMEs must identify the *anticipated* job end results and tasks. This is often referred to as a 'future-oriented job analysis' or 'strategic job analysis' (Schneider and Konz, 1989). SMEs may foresee technological changes which will alter the way in which particular job tasks are accomplished, and competencies required of those to be hired must reflect this change. Alternatively, SMEs may foresee a significant shift in the way business is conducted, requiring different competencies of future employees. As in the previous case, new end results and tasks should first be identified as a preliminary step to identifying future competency requirements.

WEIGHTING COMPETENCIES

If all competencies are of approximately equal importance, that is that no one competency is more than *twice* as important as any others, treat each competency as having the same weight. If, on the other hand, some competencies are much more important than others, competencies can be numerically weighted.

The basis on which competencies are weighted depends on how they are derived. If critical incidents are used, give most weight to those competencies which have the greatest number of critical incidents and contain critical incidents most crucial to the job. If competencies are inferred from tasks, weight most heavily those competencies which are associated with tasks rated as most important/frequent and are required for several different tasks.

A weighting scale of one to five provides an adequate range, where five represents the most important competency. Once the most important competency is weighted at five, others are compared to it, with each getting a weight of between one and five. Some competencies might have equal weight. For example, the competencies identified as important for the job of Project Leader, Performance Management System (PMS), which is referred to in Part II E, might have the following weights:

5 – people management
4 – planning
4 – knowledge of performance management systems
3 – high work standards
4 – analytic thinking
3 – decision making
3 – verbal communication
2 – written communication

Once the job analysis has been completed, the next step in the development of the BDI is to construct the actual interview questions.

DEVELOPING INTERVIEW QUESTIONS

The crux of the behavioural description interview is a set of questions which ask candidates for examples of how they have handled situations related to the required competencies. Questions are developed to elicit behavioural descriptions in each competency. Like critical incidents, behavioural descriptions include three components: the situation the candidate faced; what the candidate did (his or her actual behaviour); the outcome. For each behavioural description sought, the interviewer begins by asking an opening question about a particular situation, and then follow-up questions which probe for the candidate's behaviour and the outcome. Opening questions are planned and written out ahead of time, while follow-up questions can either be planned or developed during the interview.

If critical incidents have been identified as part of the job analysis, they form the basis of interview questions. For example, we presented earlier a critical incident concerning a person responding abruptly to a co-worker's request for help in recovering a lost computer file. This incident might be part of a competency entitled 'staff relations'. As a lead-in question to tap the candidate's staff relations skills, the interviewer might use the incident as a basis of an interview question, asking first, *'Have there been times in your present position when a co-worker has asked for help with something which was not really your responsibility?'* Assuming that the candidate says *'yes'*, the interviewer might then ask, *'What was the most recent incident you remember?'* Once the candidate has begun describing a situation, the interviewer may follow up by asking questions to gain details about the situation, about the candidate's behaviour and about the outcome.

If the job analysis did not include critical incidents, interview questions are still developed for each competency, but ask about situations similar to those *likely* to be faced on the job. Assume that a position of project coordinator is developed in a manufacturing plant for the purpose of implementing a computer-controlled production process. This is a new position, so the organization is unable to identify critical incidents for the position, hence competencies are inferred from tasks. One of the competencies identified is the ability to influence others over whom the project coordinator will have no direct control. The following question is developed to assess this competency: *'Can you think of a time where you met resistance to something you were trying to accomplish through others?'*

The sequence of questions to elicit a behavioural description typically starts broadly, and finishes with follow-up questions to get the candidate to provide specific details about the situation, behaviour, and outcome. The opening question is often used to confirm that the candidate has had experience in a particular area, for example, *'Most managers have had to discipline a staff member at some time. Have you faced such a situation?'*

Examples of BDI questions for common competencies are listed in Part II F. We recommend that you refer to this list when developing your own questions.

Generally, opening questions should not disclose to candidates the desired competency, in order to minimize candidates depicting their behaviour in light of what they believe will impress interviewers. Instead, opening questions should focus on the *situation*, and not the type of response made by the candidate or the outcome. Assume that you were developing BDI questions to assess empathy for a customer service job. Rather than asking, *'Can you think of a situation in your last retail job when you have had to show empathy to a customer?'*, ask about specific customer situations which require empathy without mentioning 'empathy', such as '*In your last retail job I assume you must have dealt with upset customers at times, can you think of a particularly difficult situation?*' You will have already identified such situations if you used a critical incident job analysis. If competencies were inferred from tasks, you will need to imagine job situations which will require the competency. Once the candidate has confirmed that he/she has had experience with such situations, the interviewer directs the candidate to *one* particular situation, often by using a focusing adjective (such as, most recent, most memorable, most challenging, most difficult, most disappointing, largest).

This concentration on actual situations which the candidate has faced is the key distinction between the BDI and the traditional, unstructured interview. Focusing on specific situations makes it more difficult for candidates to 'shade' information and to say simply what they believe will impress the interviewer by speaking in generalizations ('*I always listen to staff when they have a ccomplaint*') by giving opinions ('*I believe that the first step in dealing with staff complaints is to listen*'), or speaking hypothetically ('*If I were faced with a person who had a complaint, the first thing I would do is let the person do the talking*'). By asking about a particular past incident, the interviewer is more likely to tap what the candidate has *actually* done rather than what the candidate thinks *should* be done. After a candidate has provided details of one specific incident, the interviewer might ask for other examples.

TAILORING QUESTIONS

Identical questions need not be asked of all candidates in the BDI, and so questions can be tailored to the particular experiences of each applicant, so long as everyone has been asked for behavioural descriptions in all competency areas. After reading a candidate's résumé, an interviewer might tailor the 'generic' question, '*Can you give me an example of a major plan you developed?*' in the following way:

Interviewer: *I see that in your most recent position you coordinated the implementation of two new computer systems; did these involve much planning on your part?*

Candidate: *Yes.*

Interviewer: *Which of these involved the most planning?*

Candidate: *The Acme system.*

Interviewer: *What aspects of that system?*

Similarly, the interviewer might tailor a planned question based on what the candidate has said earlier in the interview. Imagine that a candidate has described his planning of the Acme system early in the interview, when the interviewer was dealing with the 'planning and organizing' competency. Later in the interview, when the interviewer has planned to ask about a situation in which the candidate has experienced conflict with a co-worker, the candidate might be asked, *'Earlier, you mentioned that you and a software engineer strongly disagreed over the way an aspect of the Acme system be customized. Could you tell me more about that situation?'*

Questions can also be modified for candidates who lack related work experience, such as recent graduates and people returning to work. A college recruiter interviewing for management trainee positions and wishing to tap graduating students' managerial behaviours might ask for examples of activities and groups they have led while at college. Similarly, an applicant for a supervisory position in a fast food store who has worked in the home for the past ten years might be asked about situations which required the coordination of numerous tasks to tap planning and organizing skills.

The flexibility to tailor BDI questions to particular candidates is why the BDI has sometimes been referred to as a 'patterned' interview; the interviewer follows a pattern of questions rather than asking identical questions. The main advantages of this flexibility are that a skilled interviewer can help the candidate concentrate on past experiences to recall any relevant behavioural descriptions, and it makes the interview seem less stilted. Some organizations which implement BDIs keep all questions *identical* for all candidates, believing that this practice makes the interview more fair.

In most cases, interviewers have also short-listed candidates through résumés or job applications, and tailoring BDI questions to particular candidates based on this information makes for a more comfortable and informal exchange in the interview. Interestingly, a recent study looking at ways of enhancing the structured interview indicated that structured interviews had even greater validity when interviewers had *no* prior knowledge about candidates (Searcy et al., 1993). The researchers interpreted this finding in terms of the potential biasing effect that prior information about candidates may have on interviewers. Unless an organization has sufficient personnel selection staff to dedicate two separate groups to screening and interviewing candidates, this strategy is not likely to be practical.

ASKING ABOUT BOTH POSITIVE AND NEGATIVE BEHAVIOURAL DESCRIPTIONS

Most BDI questions invite candidates to describe how they have responded to relatively neutral situations, for example, '... *your most recent sales presentation*'. Candidates will respond to such questions by describing situations in which they believe they have performed well and which have generally led to favourable outcomes. Questions can also be asked which elicit situations with less favourable outcomes. Candidates might also be asked to describe a particularly difficult sales presentation, or one which did not have a favourable outcome.

If questions which elicit possible negative behavioural descriptions are used, they should be outnumbered by neutral or positive questions and positioned *after* neutral/positive questions, in order to minimize candidates feeling intimidated. For example, a sales candidate might first be asked for a couple of behavioural descriptions of sales presentations made in the past (worded neutrally), to which the candidate describes successful presentations. These questions might then be followed by a request for a presentation which was not quite so successful. Having discussed successful presentations, the candidate will not be so uncomfortable discussing a failure.

In order to prevent candidates responding to a request for an unsuccessful situation with '*that's never happened to me*', interviewers can preface their question by implying that virtually everyone has had such experiences, '*We've all made sales presentations that did not go as well as we had expected, can you give me an example of one which you were disappointed with?*'

ASKING ABOUT DAY-TO-DAY ACTIVITIES

Some competencies apply to day-to-day activities, such as, time management and day-to-day supervision. Determining how a candidate has performed these functions does not fit the situation-behaviour-outcome framework we have discussed so far because there are no individual 'situations' which can be referred to. Nevertheless, the general principle of gaining specific details about what candidates have done can still apply by pinpointing a recent time period to ask about, such as, '*Tell me how you organized your time **yesterday**.*'

REVIEWING QUESTIONS

Before the interviews, all questions should be reviewed, preferably by someone knowledgeable about BDIs but independent of those who have developed the interview questions. Several review criteria must be kept in mind (Pursell, Campion and Gaylord, 1980):

○ Only job requirements which are important should be included in the interview.

○ Questions must be unambiguous and clearly job-related; the job analysis should ensure this.

○ Only competencies which are needed for entry to the job should be assessed; those which can be acquired through training should not be evaluated during the selection interview.

○ Questions should be reviewed to eliminate unwanted biases, such as, gender, age or ethnic discrimination.

References

Flanagan, J.C. (1954), 'The Critical Incident Technique', *Psychological Bulletin*, **51**, 327–58.

Janz, T. (1982), 'Initial Comparisons of Patterned Behavior Description Interviews Versus Unstructured Interviews', *Journal of Applied Psychology*, **67**, 577–80.

Pursell, E.D., Campion, M.A., and Gaylord, S.R. (1980), 'Structured Interviewing: Avoiding Selection Problems', *Personnel Journal*, November, 907–12.

Schneider, B. and Konz, A.M. (1989), 'Strategic Job Analysis', *Human Resource Management*, **28** (1), 51–63.

Searcy, C.A., Woods, P.N., Gatewood, R. and Lance, C. (1993), 'The Validity of Structured Interviews: A Meta-Analytical Search for Moderators'. Paper presented at the Society of Industrial Psychologists 1993 Annual Meeting, San Francisco, CA.

US Department of Labor, Employment and Training Administration (1977), *Dictionary of Occupational Titles,* (4th edn), Washington, DC: US Government Printing Office.

4

CONDUCTING THE BEHAVIOURAL DESCRIPTION INTERVIEW

❖

Most of the BDI interview consists of the interviewer asking prepared questions to elicit candidates' relevant behavioural descriptions. During this period, interviewers must ask many follow-up questions to obtain specific details about behavioural descriptions. Each of these areas is discussed below.

CONDUCTING INTERVIEWS

ASKING FOLLOW-UP QUESTIONS

While seeking behavioural descriptions, the interviewer must ask follow-up questions to gain sufficient detail about the situation faced, what the candidate did, and the outcome, as well as record behavioural descriptions. When first conducting a BDI, interviewers typically prepare both opening and follow-up questions, and ask questions exactly as they have written them down. Experienced BDI interviewers often prepare only the opening questions, and develop follow-up questions extemporaneously while conducting the interview. They also reword the opening questions as necessary to tailor them to the particular experience of each candidate.

Early in an interview, follow-up questions are required to help candidates focus on specific incidents, rather than responding with generalizations. The interviewer's first question to a candidate may concern a recent instance in which the candidate had to manage a project team. Instead of describing a specific example, the candidate describes how he or she *generally* tries to manage projects. The interviewer must then ask a follow-up

33

question to draw out the candidate on a specific instance, '*It sounds as though you have managed a number of projects involving groups of people. Can you describe the most recent project you have managed which has involved a project team?*' Let candidates know when they are specific about past experiences, by saying something like, '*That's good – just the level of detail I was looking for*'. Once candidates learn that the interviewer wants specific instances, such follow-up questions are often unnecessary.

Candidates sometimes recall an incident which is unrelated to the competencies interviewers are concentrated on. If the description fits another competency which the interviewer was planning to ask about later in the interview, encourage the candidate to go on. If, however, the situation fits neither the competency currently being asked about nor any other relevant competency, redirect the candidate by restating and clarifying the question.

Finally, follow-up questions are also used to gain additional details about the situation the candidate faced, his/her behaviour, and the outcome. For instance, after gaining sufficient details about a situation, the interviewer usually moves on to the candidate's behaviour by asking, '*And what did you do?*' or '*How did you respond?*' Avoid asking questions that imply that the candidate handled situations successfully. Ask '*What did you do?*' rather than '*How did you handle it?*' And ask '*What was the outcome?*' or '*What happened?*' or '*What was the result?*' rather than '*And was the outcome successful?*'

Generally, use open-ended follow-up questions, which require more than a one-word response ('*And what did you do when the technician said the product won't be ready for another week?*'), rather than a closed-ended question which leads the candidate ('*And did you tell the technician that one week was unacceptable?*').

RECORDING CANDIDATES' BEHAVIOURAL DESCRIPTIONS

In behavioural description interviews, judgements about the candidate's suitability for the job are withheld until after the interview, to minimize the contamination of data gathering by premature judgement. Therefore, interviewers must record the candidate's behavioural descriptions during the interview, for later analysis. While novice interviewers often mistakenly believe that they will remember what is said during an interview, experienced interviewers realize how little is actually remembered – even immediately after an interview has been completed.

Interviewers often record candidates' behavioural descriptions on notepaper during the interview. Explain at the start of the interview that you will need to take notes in order to remember the candidate's past experience. Alternatively, a tape recorder can be used. Tape-recording the interview offers the advantage of freeing you to just ask questions and provides a detailed record of what was actually said, which can be useful when deciding between two candidates with similarly high performance. However, tape-recording the interview also has a few drawbacks. The candidate may be uncomfortable with the interview being recorded, plus additional time is required after the interview to play back and transcribe behavioural descriptions after the interview.

Notes need only be taken on candidates' responses to the behavioural description questions. For each behavioural description provided by the candidate, notes should include the situation faced, the candidate's behaviour, and the outcome. Usually, only a few key words or a phrase for each of these is necessary because the interviewer will have time to review and add to these notes immediately after the interview.

It may be helpful to write the labels 'situation', 'behaviour' and 'outcome' in your interview guide, under each behavioural description question, to remind you to be sure to note these and ask follow-up questions if they are not provided by the candidate. With some experience, you may decide to omit the labels on the interview guide and simply label candidates' responses as they are provided ('S' for situation, 'B' for behaviour, 'O' for outcome).

INTERVIEW QUESTIONS TO AVOID IN A BDI

The BDI provides a framework for interview questions, focusing on actual situations candidates have faced, how they have responded to those situations, and what their outcomes have been. In our experience, there are three questions that people learning BDIs often ask which are inconsistent with the BDI framework: '*What would you have done differently?*'; '*What would you do if you were in such a situation?*'; '*What would you say is your greatest strength/weakness?*' Let us explain our concerns with these questions and offer alternatives.

The first question, about what the candidate would have done differently, usually follows the candidate sharing something he or she has done which was unsuccessful. The interviewer reasons that credit should be given to the candidate who demonstrates an understanding of a more effective way to have responded to the situation. But should the person who now sees a more effective action be given the same credit as someone who *did* perform effectively when facing a similar situation? This type of question looks more like a situational question, not a behavioural description question.

The second question, concerning what the candidate would do if in such a situation, is usually a response to the candidate saying that he or she cannot think of a particular situation that fits the interviewer's original question. Like the first, this question is hypothetical – what the candidate would do now if faced with a particular situation – and is difficult to judge objectively. (The situational interview, discussed in Chapter 5, uses hypothetical situations, but uses them with a predetermined scoring key which reduces subjectivity in judging candidate responses.)

When the candidate has difficulty thinking of a past situation, either give more time to think, acknowledging that it is often difficult to remember specific situations; make your question broader; or move on to another question. An example of broadening the question is the following. Assume that you have asked the candidate to describe a situation in which he/she has had an angry customer, but the candidate says he/she has never been in a retail position. You might reword your question by asking if the candidate has ever faced a situation in which he/she has had to respond to a co-worker or supervisor who was angry. If the candidate still cannot think of a behavioural description for a question after it has been worded more broadly, move on to another question, and consider revisiting the missed question later in the interview. The candidate may later remember an incident, often triggered by the description of incidents for other questions. In many cases, however, candidates do not have any experience of some job-related situations, and will not be judged as favourably in those areas as others who do. (Further discussion about how candidates are judged is presented later in this chapter.)

The third question, what the candidate believes to be his or her greatest strengths and weaknesses, is one of the most frequently asked questions in the traditional unstructured interview, and some experienced interviewers want to include it in structured interviews. It fits with neither the BDI nor the situational interview discussed in Chapter 5 because it is not based on job-related competencies and it is not behavioural. Thus the evaluation of responses is too prone to interviewer biases developed earlier in the interview. If a 'strength' is required for the job, it should be asked about through a planned behavioural description question.

Similarly, it is difficult to judge objectively what a candidate says about weaknesses. Is the candidate who discloses a major weakness discredited for having the weakness or credited for honesty? There is too much room with such a question for interviewer biases to affect the judgement of answers. Finally, most job candidates who have read a book or attended a class on how to make a favourable impression in a job interview have learned that they are likely to be asked about their strengths and weaknesses. They have been told in these books and sessions to make a weakness a strength by claiming to have a weakness that the interviewer would really want in an employee anyway, such as '*Colleagues and friends often tell me that I take my job too seriously*' or '*I guess I'm a bit too much of a perfectionist*'.

THE BDI INTERVIEW GUIDE

Once all BDI questions have been determined and how interviews will be opened and closed has been decided, a complete interview guide should be developed and used in each interview.

The amount of detail included in the guide is up to each interviewer or organization. Minimally, questions to elicit behavioural descriptions for each competency should be written on the interview guide. Additional detail might be included, depending on individual interviewers' preferences and the extent to which the organization wishes to maintain interview structure.

More experienced interviewers generally require less detail than those using the BDI approach for the first time. For example, new interviewers often detail what they will say to open and close the interview, while more experienced interviewers do this without notes. Similarly, some interviewers list follow-up questions they will ask to draw out behaviours and outcomes for each behavioural description question, while others might list only the initial question which is used to elicit relevant situations from candidates.

While new interviewers may wish to list both initial and follow-up questions for the interview, there is a danger in doing so of making the interview too rigid and in the interviewer losing too much eye contact with the candidate from having to constantly refer to the interview guide. Our preference is to list on the interview guide only the question to elicit the situation faced, leaving the interviewer to extemporaneously develop follow-up questions as needed. We favour this approach for two reasons. First, as we mentioned earlier, too many questions on the interview guide can make the interview unnecessarily stiff. Second, follow-up questions need to be based on what the candidate says in order to keep the interview on track. If the candidate fails to provide a specific situation, the first follow-up question should be to concentrate the candidate's attention on an actual situation. If the candidate presents a specific situation, but fails to provide sufficient detail about it, the first follow-up questions should elicit more details. Alternatively, the candidate might provide sufficient details about the situation so that the first logical follow-up question would be about what the candidate did (behaviour). The candidate might even describe both the situation and what he/she did, requiring only a follow-up question about the outcome. In other words, appropriate fol-low-up questions will depend on what the candidate says, and can only be planned in a very general way.

For these reasons we suggest that, while some interviewers might pre-fer to list a series of follow-up questions for each principal question, the interview guide should generally be limited to only the initial question. An interview guide that includes only one question for each situation requires the interviewer to be skilled in generating appropriate follow-up ques-tions on the spot. This skill can be developed with practice, and any train-ing programme designed to teach how to conduct BDIs should include opportunities for all participants to practise and receive feedback on using follow-up questions. (BDI training programmes are discussed in Chapter 6.)

Examples of BDI interview guides for three different jobs can be found in Part II G. The first, 'Project Leader, Performance Management System (PMS)', was developed by inferring competencies from tasks, since it was a new position and no critical incidents could be obtained for it. You may wish to refer also to Part II C, D and E, which are based on this same job. The other two jobs, 'Government Planner/Analyst' and 'Hospital Charge Nurse', were existing positions, and so critical incidents were used to develop competencies and interview questions (listed before each inter-view guide).

To avoid redundancy, we have included how the interview will be opened and closed, and the labels 'Situation', 'Behaviour' and 'Outcome' under each BDI question, for only the first job (Project Leader, PMS). However, in practice, the latter two jobs would also include this informa-tion. The labels for each component of the behavioural description (situa-tion, behaviour, outcome) help remind new interviewers to use follow-up questions to obtain complete behavioural descriptions. More experienced behavioural description interviewers may wish to omit these labels.

RATING CANDIDATES AND MAKING THE SELECTION DECISION

After completing a behavioural description interview, you must have time to review notes (or tape recordings), and to judge the candidate based on behavioural descriptions provided. Assuming that the interviewer has taken notes, time to review notes should be scheduled *immediately* after the interview.

While reviewing notes, reconcile any gaps or inconsistencies in infor-mation, making sure that each behavioural description is labelled with the competency it reflects. Some behavioural descriptions reflect behaviour in more than one competency, and should be labelled as such.

Ratings can either be made on individual competencies first, before a final judgement or rating of the candidate is made, or on a global basis, in which the candidate's performance is judged over the entire interview at once. We recommend the former, because it is less likely to allow extraneous factors to affect interviewers' judgements.

Competency ratings are based on the behavioural descriptions given by the candidate for each competency – typically two or three. How highly a candidate is rated on a competency should depend on:

○ how *relevant* the situations in the behavioural descriptions are to those which would be faced on the job;
○ the *effectiveness of the candidate's behaviour* (how closely it matches effective behaviour indicated by the competency);
○ how *many* behavioural descriptions were given for a particular competency; and
○ how *recent* the behavioural descriptions are.

Of these four considerations, the first two (*relevance* and *effectiveness of behaviour*) are the most important. Consider a person applying for a sales position which involves selling expensive, mainframe computer systems. The candidate has been in many sales situations, but all have been in retail stores, usually involving electronics items of less than $500 value. The sales experience is somewhat relevant, but clearly not as relevant as having sold more expensive items, and computer systems in particular.

The candidate's *behaviour* in those sales situations is also critical, which is why it is important when seeking behavioural descriptions to probe what the candidate actually did. Assume that one of the competencies for the target position is listening and uncovering specific customer needs. A candidate could have extensive sales experience, but when probed for how sales were made, it may be discovered that the person did little to uncover needs. Related to the effectiveness of the candidate's behaviour is the outcome of each behavioural description. Assuming that effective behaviours were used, outcomes are likely to be positive as well. Note, however, that outcomes are often affected by circumstances outside the individual's control.

Other things being equal, we can assume that the candidate who has had *many* relevant experiences has a better chance of succeeding on the job than those with fewer. The person who has made many sales presentations in the past is more likely to succeed in a sales position. Finally, the most *recent* experiences and behaviour carry more weight than those in the past because the more recent the behaviour, the better predictor it is of future behaviour.

Competency ratings are typically made on scales from one to five, and can be anchored either by how the candidate compares with the competency required in the job, or by how the candidate compares with other candidates. If a five-point rating scale is used to compare candidates to the level of competency required of the job, the following anchors can be used:

1 – far below minimum requirements
2 – marginally below minimum requirements
3 – just meets minimum requirements
4 – marginally above minimum requirements
5 – far above minimum requirements

A common five-point rating scale used to reflect candidates' performance relative to other candidates' performance typically has anchors reflecting percentile rank, such as:

1 – candidate's performance is in the lowest 20 per cent of all candidates
2 – 20–40 per cent
3 – 40–60 per cent
4 – 60–80 per cent
5 – 80–100 per cent

We strongly recommend a comparison of the candidate with the job requirements (the first scale) for two reasons. First, it avoids the potential problem of offering a position to the best of a group of candidates who all fall short of meeting minimum job requirements. Our second reason is a logistical concern. Each candidate should be evaluated as soon as possible after the interview while the interviewer still remembers well what the candidate said. (Even though the interviewer has notes, they are only abbreviations of what was actually said in the interview.) However, candidates cannot really be rated in comparison to others until *all* candidates have been interviewed, except when interviews are conducted for many similar positions (such as, a new plant start-up), and a large number of previous candidates can serve as the comparison group. Therefore, using a rating system which compares candidates to each other requires one of the following three scenarios in most cases: ratings are not made until all candidates have been interviewed (meaning that candidates interviewed early are rated some time after their interviews); all but the last candidate are rated in comparison to what interviewers *anticipate* other candidates' performance to be; all interviews are tape-recorded and played back at the time of rating. We see none of these alternatives as optimal, and so we favour a comparison of candidates with job requirements.

If there are several interviewers, each interviewer should *individually* rate candidates on each competency, before discussing candidates' performance with other interviewers. This practice minimizes one interviewer influencing others' preliminary ratings. After individual interviewers have written their own ratings, ratings of all interviewers can be integrated either through consensus or by simply averaging ratings across interviewers. In their research on structured interviews, Wiesner and Cronshaw (1988) compared the validity of consensus versus averaging approaches to the integration of interviewers' ratings, and found higher validity with the consensus approach, and so we recommend using the consensus technique. Part II H provides a sample form for integrating interviewers' ratings using consensus.

Once consensus or average ratings have been established for each candidate on each competency, a final selection decision can be made. Assuming that ratings are anchored to job requirements (that is, 3 corresponds with 'just meets minimum requirements'), check that top-performing candidates score at least a '3' on each important competency. If not, the position might have to be readvertised or aspects of the job (such as, compensation package) may need to be changed in order to attract a minimally qualified applicant pool.

If competencies have been treated as having equal weight, candidates can be compared with each other by summing competency ratings for each candidate. In cases where two or more top candidates have about equal ratings, a final decision can be made by considering trainability of the lower rating competencies for each individual. Assume that two candidates each have total ratings of 25 across seven competencies, with about the same ratings on all but two competencies: Candidate A is lower on technical knowledge while candidate B is lower on team management. Candidate A might be selected over B if the technical knowledge is believed to be more easily trained on the job than is team management. If, on the other hand, there are *no* differences between the two candidates on individual competencies, further information needs to be gathered to make a final decision, for instance through additional interviews or reference checks. If competencies have been weighted, these weights can be combined with competency ratings by multiplying weights and ratings, and summing weighted ratings, as in Part II I.

In most cases, candidates are interviewed for only one (or a few) vacant positions, and so the selection decision is usually a matter of choosing the best performing candidate, as has been outlined above. In some cases, however, structured interviews are part of a selection procedure for large-scale hiring, such as in a new production plant start-up. In these situations, cut-off scores are an alternative to hiring from the top down.

A cut-off score approach to personnel selection means that all candidates who achieve a particular score are either hired, or may proceed to the next phase of the selection process. When multiple selection methods are used, cut-off scores can be established for each method, or for all but one method. In general, a cut-off score approach is most appropriate when it is believed that people doing the job must have a minimum level of competency, but that having more than that minimum level is likely to make little difference in job performance.

The setting of cut-off scores is a somewhat arbitrary judgement, based on a number of factors which are beyond the scope of this book. In the case of BDIs, with a five-point rating scale based on a comparison to job requirements, a logical cut-off score is an average of a rating of 3 ('just meets minimum requirements'), or a minimum of a 3 rating in all important competencies.

COMMON CONCERNS ABOUT BEHAVIOURAL DESCRIPTION INTERVIEWS

In our experience of teaching managers and personnel specialists how to conduct BDIs, three concerns have been raised. First, *BDIs usually take longer to prepare and to conduct than unstructured interviews.* This point is usually raised by personnel specialists, anticipating resistance from line managers about spending the additional time. It is true that unstructured interviews typically take less time than BDIs. Unstructured interviewers often ask many of the same questions of candidates, regardless of the position being applied for, and so preparation time may be negligible. Unstructured interviews often last between 20 and 50 minutes, while structured interviews can take an hour or more. Our response to this concern is to emphasize the importance of the personnel selection decision. The benefit to the organization of picking the best of a group of applicants lasts for the tenure of the individual in that organization, which in our view more than justifies the extra couple of hours preparing for and conducting a BDI.

The second concern has been that *BDIs advantage people with work experience over recent graduates and people who have been out of the workforce for some time.* It is true that people who have extensive work experience are likely to have more relevant behavioural descriptions (provided they are applying for a position which matches their past work experience), but they will not necessarily demonstrate more effective *behaviours* in those situations, which is also a criterion for evaluating candidates in the BDI. When candidates do not have much relevant work-related experience, interviewers can ask more broadly about relevant experience, including non-work-related situations in which target competencies could have been demonstrated.

Finally, some interviewers have raised a concern that *individuals might learn that they will receive a BDI, and if so will prepare for it and have an advantage over those who do not.* This situation is most likely for internal applicants who apply for promotion in an organization which has adopted a BDI approach to interviewing. In general, people who prepare for *any* type of interview or test have a better chance of succeeding with it than those who do not. But because the BDI deals with actual past experiences, the only advantage to those who have prepared is the additional time to remember relevant past situations.

BDIs are the most common form of structured employment interview because they can be used flexibly, for filling from one position to many positions. In the next chapter, we describe an alternative approach, the situational interview.

References

Wiesner, W.H. and Cronshaw, S.F. (1988), 'A Meta-Analytic Investigation of the Impact of Interview Format and Degree of Structure on the Validity of the Employment Interview', *Journal of Occupational Psychology*, **61**, 275–90.

5

THE SITUATIONAL INTERVIEW

❖

S ituational interviews for personnel selection were first introduced in 1980 by Gary Latham and his colleagues from the University of Washington and the Weyerhaeuser Company in North Carolina, USA. As has been discussed in Chapters 2 and 3, numerous problems with conventional unstructured interviews led researchers and human resource practitioners to look for alternative interview methods which might prove more reliable, valid and fair in the selection of employees. Like BDIs, situational interviews were developed to address these three main issues: the ability to consistently identify people who can do the job; the ability to make selection decisions which are capable of withstanding legal scrutiny; practicality in implementation (Latham, 1989).

BASIC ASSUMPTIONS

Like BDIs, the situational approach deals with specific behaviours, rather than global attributes or 'traits' of the person. However, whereas BDIs are based on the premise that past behaviour is the best predictor of future behaviour, the situational interview was derived from a theory of motivation known as goal setting theory (Locke, 1968).

In simple terms, goal setting theory suggests that a person's future behaviours are strongly influenced by his or her behavioural intentions or goals. Using this assumption, the purpose of the situational interview is to identify job candidates' work-related behavioural intentions by presenting them with a series of incidents which might occur on the job and for each one asking: '*What would you do in this situation?*' It is assumed that what individuals say they would do will correspond closely with their actual future behaviour. For example, if a candidate for a supervisory position suggests that she would consult widely with her superiors before making important decisions, it is anticipated that is in fact how she would behave in situations which require these kinds of decisions.

Clearly a critical feature of situational interview questions is their focus on tapping meaningful samples of behaviour. Put another way, situational questions will be valid to the extent that they parallel events which actually occur on the job. The closer they reflect real-life situations, the more likely these questions will predict future job performance. As we have seen earlier with conventional unstructured interviews, a major reason for their lack of validity is that they frequently address issues and topics that are irrelevant to the job. Situational interviews attempt to overcome that limitation by concentrating only on job-relevant incidents.

There are, of course, other methods of personnel selection which also assess job-related activities. Work samples and assessment centres, for example, provide an opportunity for job candidates to demonstrate skills and competencies which they would be required to display in the work context. These activities are described as 'high fidelity' simulations of job behaviour, because they very closely mimic actual behaviours expected on the job. (*See* Chapter 6 for a review of these approaches.) These methods are very useful for selection purposes but they can also be very costly to develop and to implement, particularly in terms of time. Situational interviews offer an efficient and less costly method of simulating potential work-related incidents and exploring how job candidates would react to them. This 'low fidelity' approach entails presenting a verbal description of a hypothetical work incident and asking job candidates how they might deal with it.

The following is an illustration of a situational interview question used in the selection of nurses in a hospital setting:

> You are concerned about one of your patients. You believe his condition is worsening and that the house-surgeon is not ordering appropriate treatment. You have discussed your concerns with the doctor, but he has dismissed them. What would you do in this situation?

This example contains all the basic elements of a typical situational question. There is a brief outline of an incident which has occurred ('*the patient is not doing well; the doctor is not providing needed treatment; you have raised your concerns but they have not been heeded*'), followed by the question: '*What would you do?*' All that remains is to 'score' the acceptability of candidates' answers. Procedures for constructing situational questions and for evaluating job candidates' responses are outlined below.

DEVELOPING THE SITUATIONAL INTERVIEW

In general, situational interviews are developed by identifying specific activities that are representative of the job and then constructing questions around this information to ask job candidates. Specific procedures are listed below, and summarized in Figure 5.1. We suggest that you refer to Part II J, which provides an example of a complete situational interview, as you read these procedures.

As with a BDI, the first step in developing a situational interview is to conduct a job analysis. Unlike BDIs, however, a situational interview cannot be developed by inferring competencies from tasks; it requires a critical incident job analysis. Since critical incidents are necessary, situational interviews are not appropriate for new jobs, jobs that have been changed significantly, and jobs in which there have been only one or two incumbents in the past. (*See* Chapter 3 for instructions on conducting a critical incident job analysis.) As with critical incidents used for BDIs, critical incidents for situational interviews are grouped into competencies by SMEs, and weighted if any one competency is more than twice the importance of another.

DEVELOPING SITUATIONAL INTERVIEW QUESTIONS

Once competencies have been determined, SMEs construct 2 or 3 interview questions for each competency from the critical incidents identified. For most competencies, there are more than 2 or 3 critical incidents – each a potential basis for an interview question – and so the list of critical incidents must be reduced. Select critical incidents for situational interview questions which most clearly represent the competency, and which, when turned into situational interview questions, are likely to produce a *range* of responses from candidates, some more effective than others, so that the questions will serve to distinguish candidates from one another.

Each incident is reworded in terms of an interview question which can be posed to all the job candidates for the position. This is usually not difficult, requiring only a description of the selected incident, followed by the question: '*What would you do in this situation?*' Using the supervisory position as an example, a typical question might be: '*One of your subordinates has misunderstood your instructions and incorrectly completed a task which you assigned to him. This has caused a serious problem in your section. What would you do?*'

FIGURE 5.1   STEPS FOR CONDUCTING A SITUATIONAL
INTERVIEW

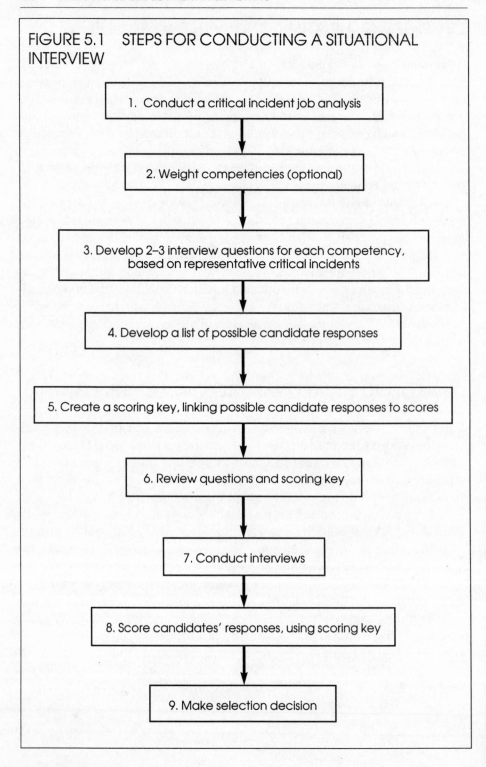

DEVELOPING AN ANSWER SCORING KEY FOR EACH QUESTION

Having developed the questions to be asked of job candidates, the next step in the procedure is to derive a method of 'scoring' their responses to these questions. This is important for ensuring agreement among interviewers as to what constitutes an appropriate versus inappropriate response. Without a predetermined scoring key, interviewers' judgements of candidates' responses are prone to be contaminated by initial impressions and other biases discussed earlier in Chapter 1.

For each interview question, a comprehensive list of possible candidate responses must be generated. When the number of incumbents in the target job is not large (say, less than 100), the simplest means of doing this is using a small group of SMEs, who brainstorm likely responses, either individually or as a group. When there is a large number of incumbents, an alternative approach is to survey all incumbents in the target job, asking them to describe what they would do in response to each hypothetical situation. Such a survey can be administered through either questionnaire or interview, and provides an opportunity to easily determine the concurrent, criterion-related validity of the situational interview (*see* Chapter 1). Below we explain how the incumbent response survey can be used for this purpose.

Next, possible answers to each question must be placed on a scoring scale. Incumbents and managers who are quite experienced and considered most competent should be used as SMEs to assign scores to possible answers. Typically, a five-point scale is constructed for each question, although three-point scales have also been used. On a five-point scale, a score of 1 represents an unacceptable response, 3 reflects an acceptable response, and 5 a very good response, with 2 and 4 allowing for judgements in between. Possible candidate responses are anchored to points on the scale (usually just the 5, 3 and 1 points on a five-point scale).

Judgements about the appropriateness of a job candidate's response are based upon the likely consequences of the suggested action. Interviewers will use the scoring guide to rate the appropriateness of each candidate's answers to each of the questions posed during the interview. Using the supervision example given earlier, the following scoring system might be derived:

1 = report the subordinate's failure to higher authorities
3 = fix the situation yourself
5 = work with the subordinate to rectify the situation.

For many questions, there would be several responses which are considered to be inappropriate (and should therefore be scored 1) and likewise many actions which might be worthy of a 3 or 5. The exact determination of response scoring will depend on factors such as the complexity of the situation. The critical incident job analysis and the judgements of SMEs can be used to decide how many different alternative responses might be possible and how they should be scored.

THE INCUMBENT RESPONSE SURVEY USED FOR DETERMINING THE INTERVIEW'S CRITERION-RELATED VALIDITY

We mentioned earlier that when the number of incumbents already in the job is large (at least 100), a survey of all incumbents to generate possible answers has the advantage of easily determining the interview's concurrent, criterion validity. After the job analyst has collected all incumbents' responses to the situational interview questions, responses are grouped according to their similarity with each other. A group of SMEs reviews these responses (without knowing which employees offered particular responses) and develops a scoring key for each interview question.

In order to determine the interview's concurrent, criterion-related validity, incumbents' responses to each question must be scored using the scoring key, and an overall interview score developed for each incumbent. This score serves as the 'predictor' for validation purposes. A measure of incumbents' current levels of job performance must be used as a 'criterion'. The criterion measure could be: an existing performance appraisal instrument which includes numeric ratings; objective indices of performance (such as, annual sales volume); a supervisory performance rating scale developed specifically for the purpose of validating the interview. Incumbents' predictor scores (that is, overall interview scores) are correlated with their criterion scores, which yields a concurrent, criterion-related validity coefficient.

Conducting a criterion-related validation study involves many more issues than we have described in this brief overview, and these issues go beyond the scope of the present book. For instance, the performance criterion measure used must be reliable and valid, and we have said nothing about interpreting the resulting validity coefficient in light of range restriction (that is, incumbents usually represent considerably less than the full range of candidates for a given position) and criterion unreliability. Furthermore, if such a study is conducted with a large enough number of incumbents, follow-up analyses can assess the validity of individual items. The reader interested in interview validation procedures should consult texts such as Gatewood and Feild (1990) or Cascio (1993), which provide more detailed treatments of the topic.

REVIEWING QUESTIONS

Before conducting a situational interview, questions should be reviewed for comprehensiveness, clarity, appropriateness and freedom from bias, as discussed in reference to BDIs in Chapter 3. Situational interview questions should also be reviewed to:

○ ensure that the scoring key covers virtually all possible candidates' responses;

○ eliminate any questions which might not differentiate between candidates; and

○ (if feasible) check the predictive validity of the questions and answer scoring key.

Check whether the scoring key covers virtually all possible candidate responses by pilot testing it with present incumbents or, if few incumbents are available, with others in the organization who are likely to respond to questions as candidates might. Questions can fail to differentiate between candidates for a few reasons. First, a question might be transparent to candidates, so that the 'correct' answer is immediately obvious. Similarly, it is possible that *no* candidates will give the most effective answer. If all candidates give the same answer to a question, its predictive utility is lost due to lack of a range of responses.

Alternatively, if it is not clear what is an effective behaviour in a particular situation, interviewers might not be able to agree upon what constitutes a good versus poor response, and will therefore be unable to agree upon the scoring of candidates' answers. This also undermines the validity and reliability of the scoring system. Again, a small pilot study of the interview questions will help to eliminate these potential difficulties.

If there is a large number of incumbents in the present position (about 100 or more), the validity of the questions and answer scoring keys can be checked by administering the situational interview, and correlating individual question scores with one or more measures of job performance (such as, performance appraisal ratings). The magnitude of the correlation between individual interview questions and the performance measure reflects the quality of the item in predicting performance.

Alternatively, interview question scores and performance data for actual job candidates who are hired can be correlated to assess the quality of interview questions. Both of these approaches are referred to as criterion-related validation studies. The former is called a 'concurrent' study because interview scores and performance measures are gathered at the same time, while the latter is referred to as 'predictive'. Specific techniques for conducting such studies can be found in many personnel selection texts.

CONDUCTING A SITUATIONAL INTERVIEW

A situational interview can be opened and closed in much the same way as we have described for a BDI (*see* Chapter 4). The same situational questions are asked of all candidates, typically in the same order. Interview panel members note candidates' responses during the interview for later discussion. While in some organizations panel members score answers during the interview, we recommend that they wait until after the interview. Scoring during the interview gets in the way of panel members recording actual responses, which makes it difficult for them to adequately resolve differences in scores after the interview. Candidates may also feel uncomfortable being rated while they talk.

SCORING CANDIDATES' RESPONSES AND MAKING THE SELECTION DECISION

As with BDIs, scores on each separate competency can be calculated, based on scores for the questions representing the competency. Alternatively, scores to questions can simply be added, irrespective of competencies, to arrive at a total score. If this latter approach is used, the number of questions developed for each competency will need to represent the importance (that is, weight) of that competency. For example, a very important competency might be represented by five questions, while a less important competency might be covered in two.

Where there is disagreement between interviewers on the score to be assigned to a candidate on a particular competency, this is discussed until consensus is reached. If candidates are scored on each competency, forms for integrating several interviewers' ratings can be used (Part II H and I).

RELIABILITY AND VALIDITY OF THE SITUATIONAL INTERVIEW

Although situational interviews are still relatively new, there have been several studies of both their reliability and their validity. Research on *reliability* has concentrated mainly on the extent to which interviewers agree with each other in their judgements about job candidates. Agreement among interviewers, which is one major form of reliability we wish to establish, can be easily calculated. When each member of the interview panel has rated each candidate on all of the behavioural competencies assessed during the interview, we compute the proportion of agreements/disagreements in the scores assigned to candidates. Various studies have found quite high between-interviewer consistency in situational interviews. In a review of research carried out during the 1980s, Latham (1989) summarized evidence showing that inter-observer consistency ranged from around 76 per cent to 96 per cent, an impressive record for this type of interview.

Using a somewhat different approach, Maurer and Fay (1988) examined *variation* between interviewers in their ratings of job candidates from situational interviews. Again the results were impressive. Even when observers were unfamiliar with the situational interview method and had been given little training in how to use the technique, the extent of variability was quite low, and significantly less than the amount of variation among ratings derived from conventional interviews. These findings indicate that even inexperienced 'judges' can evaluate job candidates fairly uniformly when situational interview procedures are used, and that the situational interview produces greater consistency in evaluations than the traditional, unstructured interview.

Although the *validity* of unstructured interviews has not been encouraging, the validity of the situational interview has been well established in recent research. Most studies have obtained validity estimates which are well in excess of those obtained for traditional, unstructured interviews, and are comparable to those obtained for cognitive ability testing and assessment centres, which are generally more costly and difficult to develop and use (Latham, 1989). Predictive validity, which estimates the relationship between scores on the selection procedure and later job performance, has been found to be around 0.40.

The one exception to these positive findings occurred in an early study by Latham and Saari (1984), where a correlation of just 0.14 was found between interview scores and performance appraisals conducted three years later by the appointees' supervisors. This unexpectedly low correlation led the researchers to explore more closely how the interviews had actually been conducted. It turned out that, in several cases, the original interviewers had not adhered correctly to the situational interview procedures. In particular, rather than recording and scoring responses to each situational question, the interviewers had not recorded anything and had simply formed global impressions of candidates, which they then used as the basis for selection. In short, while they had used the situational interview technique to ask the questions, assessment of the responses had reverted back to the traditional approach of making general judgements, rather than using the actual scores obtained by job candidates on each behavioural competency.

The Latham and Saari study underlines the importance of following the scoring guide which has been developed for use with situational questions. In particular, each behavioural competency must be assessed independently of other competencies, to avoid the effects of first impressions, halo and other biases which distort global impressions. Correct usage of the procedure in its entirety is necessary to ensure high validity in the prediction of future job performance.

Finally, a recent study conducted by Stohr-Gilmore and her colleagues (Stohr-Gilmore, Stohr-Gilmore and Kistler, 1990) compared the outcomes of interviews in which situational questions were utilized with those in which more traditional interview questions were asked and no situational questions were included. Correlations between interview assessments of candidates for the position of correction officer in a county jail and their later performance on the job were considerably higher when situational questions were included in the selection interview than when they were not, again highlighting the validity of the situational approach.

Several explanations can be proffered for the success of the situational interview. First, attention is on specific behaviour, rather than vague personality attributes or traits, and anchored rating scales are used for recording behavioural information. Latham (1989) has suggested that situational questions based on job analysis are realistic samples of work behaviour and are similar to the types of situations which candidates might confront in the work setting. Obviously, correspondence between the issues explored during the selection interview and actual job conditions will increase the ability of the interview to predict job performance.

Second, it has been cogently argued (by Latham and others) that job-related behavioural intentions can serve as accurate indicators of how an individual will actually behave on the job. Asking job candidates how they would act in relation to specific job-relevant situations can provide a valid index of how they will behave in those situations. In this context, what people say they will do can indeed correspond with what they will actually do.

A further explanation of the correlation between situational interview responses and job performance relates to behavioural consistency (Motowidlo, Dunnette and Carter, 1990). When individuals are asked what they would do in a particular situation, they may try to recall what they have done in the past in similar circumstances. Hence their responses to situational questions may, in fact, be a reflection of their past behaviour. This is similar to arguments presented by social psychologist Daryl Bem (1972) about the relationship between people's attitudes and their behaviour. Bem suggested that individuals make judgements about themselves by examining how they have behaved previously and then inferring their attitudes and values from these observations of their own behaviours. In the same way, it is feasible that future behavioural intentions might be decided by reflecting on one's responses to similar incidents in previous work situations.

COMPARISON OF SITUATIONAL INTERVIEWS WITH BDIs

As outlined in Chapter 3, BDIs rest on a somewhat different assumption, namely that past behaviour will predict future behaviour. That is, knowledge of how a person has acted in previous situations will give us the best forecast of how that person will respond in future, similar circumstances. Hence BDI questions deal with previous experiences of job candidates, asking individuals what they have done in various situations. One potential limitation of this approach, however, is that some job candidates may not have encountered experiences relevant to those focused upon in the interview and will therefore not have had an opportunity to engage in relevant behaviours (Latham et al., 1980; Weekly and Gier, 1987). When this happens, in BDIs the candidate will be given a score of zero on those particular behavioural competencies. In this sense, BDIs disadvantage individuals who have not had the opportunity to demonstrate certain behaviours (Latham et al., 1980), and may in fact eliminate candidates who could be suitable for a position, especially an entry-level one.

Situational interviews, on the other hand, do not assume that job candidates have had experience with a particular kind of incident, only that they can make judgements about how they would behave if they did encounter such an incident. Certainly those who have confronted similar previous experiences may have the advantage of being able to reflect on what they have done in the past and be able to base their interview responses on these reflections, but in principle all job candidates have the same opportunity to respond to situational questions.

Some authors (Latham, 1989; Maurer and Fay, 1988) have suggested that situational interview questions and BDI questions may be combined in the one interview. That is, some questions could concentrate on previous experiences and others on behavioural intentions. This approach certainly has some appeal. However, Latham (1989) has raised some important issues to consider if a combined approach is adopted:

○ Are some behaviours more readily tapped via one method or the other? This would be critical to deciding whether a behavioural or situational question would be appropriate.

○ To what extent do situational interviews and BDIs yield the same conclusions about job candidates? To date, there has been no investigation which compares the selection decisions made via situational interviews with those drawn from BDIs.

O   What is the incremental validity (added accuracy) of combining sit-
     uational interviews and BDI questions? Given the costs (especially
     in time) of developing structured questions, would the joint
     approach yield better decisions than using one or other method?
     Again, at this time there has been no empirical assessment of this
     issue.

Added to these points are potential difficulties in the weighting of questions. Should a previous behaviour (elicited via a BDI question) be given
the same or greater weight than a behavioural intention tapped by a situational question? Would job candidates who are capable of answering BDI
questions, as well as situational interviews questions, achieve higher
scores than those who may not be able to answer BDI questions? If so, is
this desirable?

Clearly there are some critical issues here which require further attention. Until they are resolved, our recommendation is that personnel selec-
tors should weigh the pros and cons of situational interviews and BDIs
for their specific circumstances, and opt for one or other of these two
approaches, rather than attempting to combine them together.

BENEFITS OF SITUATIONAL INTERVIEWS

Having outlined the process of conducting situational interviews and
compared this technique with BDIs, we now examine some of the advantages to be gained from utilization of this approach. We shall then look at
some of the possible drawbacks of using situational interviews, before
concluding this chapter with some important issues relating to the use of
structured interviews in general and this type of interview in particular.

On a purely practical level, two advantages of the situational approach
are that it reduces variation due to the differing ability of interviewers to
obtain and interpret information about job candidates, and it increases the
level of agreement between interviewers in making their final selection
decisions (Maurer and Fay, 1988). The first of these is significant because
we want judgements about whether or not to employ a person to be influenced solely by candidate characteristics, not those of the interviewer.
Interviewers vary in their capacity to assimilate and evaluate information
about candidates, which can substantially reduce the reliability of the
interview as a selection method. Similarly, lack of agreement between
interviewers (which may also be due to variability between interviewers)
will have a severe negative impact on their ability to select employees
who will be successful on the job.

An important requirement noted by Latham (1989) for selection interviews is that they must be practical and readily applicable. In relation to this, Weekly and Gier (1987) asked managers in a retail chain what their impressions were of the practicality of the situational interview. Responses were overwhelmingly positive, with many mentioning 'the job-relatedness of the interview, the ease of administration, and the ease of interpretation' (Weekly and Gier, 1987, p.486). The authors commented that many of the store managers had initially expressed concerns about their ability to assess job candidates' capabilities while at the same time avoiding 'potentially troublesome interview questions' (ibid.), but these concerns were allayed once they became familiar with the situational procedure. Clearly, a critical factor in the implementation of this type of personnel interview is its acceptance by those who will be using it. Weekly and Gier's anecdotal evidence, and observations provided by other investigators, suggest that situational interviews are seen to be very practical and relatively straightforward to use, once the initial development work (in particular the job analysis) has been done.

DISADVANTAGES OF SITUATIONAL INTERVIEWS

We alluded above to the main difficulty associated with situational interviews, the costs of development. These costs come from two areas – the job analysis and development of the response scoring guide. There can be no doubt that critical incident job analysis, which is essential for the derivation of situational questions, incurs costs to the organization, both in time and energy required to complete this task. In some instances it may not be feasible to actually conduct a full-scale job analysis for an advertised position. Particularly where the organization is small and where there are just one or a few job incumbents, it may be necessary to refer to job analyses which have been carried out elsewhere on similar positions.

Fortunately, information is usually available which might assist in the development of job-relevant behavioural questions. Only where the position is essentially unique, or where it differs substantially from similar job titles in the same or other organizations, will this create a major hurdle in the process of constructing interview questions. In these circumstances, the practicality of performing a critical incident job analysis will need to be considered carefully.

Another task which is potentially time-consuming is the derivation of the answer scoring key, once the situational questions have been decided upon. It is important to ensure that the scoring system is realistic, that responses which are given a score of 1 are not so ridiculous that no candidate would mention them, while 5 responses are not too idealistic (Latham, 1989). While careful thought must be given to derivation of the scoring guide, valid systems of evaluating candidate responses are usually achievable.

Gabris and Rock (1991) have discussed another potential restriction on the utility of structured interviews. In a study of selection interview outcomes in the Mississippi Department of Corrections, they found (contrary to other studies) that the situational interview did not lead to consistent improvements in later job performance, when compared with a traditional unstructured interview. Gabris and Rock raise the interesting possibility that 'organizational culture attributes, and the socialization process, may simply overwhelm initial differences between employees' (p.477), no matter how they have been selected. In this particular organization, there were strong pressures on new employees to adopt the values and behaviour patterns of existing members of the organization. Coupled with a rigid set of behavioural norms and rules for correction officers, the opportunity for individual differences to emerge in this setting was probably very slim.

The conditions described by Gabris and Rock (1991) are not typical of most organizations, however. In most contexts it is likely that job-related behaviour will vary between individuals and that individual differences will not be 'swamped' by organizational factors, such as cultural values and socialization practices. Typically it would be anticipated that the method of selecting new employees will have a significant impact on successful job performance in the future.

FINAL REFLECTIONS

In this chapter we have outlined the rationale for utilizing situational interviews in personnel selection, the basic steps involved in conducting situational interviews, and the costs and benefits of adopting this method of interviewing. During our discussion we have highlighted some of the major factors which will influence the effectiveness of the situational approach. To conclude this discussion of situational interviews, we summarize some of its key features:

○ *Correspondence with job requirements* Questions constructed for the situational interview must be closely related to *important* job duties. In other words, situational questions must be based on behavioural requirements which are critical for successful job performance. Furthermore, given the limited time period which is normally available for selection interviews, examining behaviours which are less central to overall effectiveness on the job will reduce the capacity of the interview to discriminate between candidates on key competencies.

○ *Job analysis* Consistent with the above, situational questions must be developed from a critical incident job analysis. Otherwise, we have no guarantee that these questions will be relevant to the person's future job performance.

○ *Transparency* A major advantage of the situational interview over BDIs is that situational interviews do not require job candidates to have had prior exposure to the incidents under consideration. Given that candidates are asked to state 'what they would do', we have to construct questions in such a way that the 'right' answers are not guessable or immediately obvious to the interviewee.

○ *Assessing candidate responses* A systematic scoring guide is essential to ensure that job candidates' responses to situational questions are assessed consistently, across candidates and across interviewers. The response scoring guide must be constructed carefully, to avoid unrealistic responses (at either the low or the high end of the scale). As we noted earlier, failure to use a response scale to evaluate candidates' answers to each question will eliminate any advantage the situational interview has over the unstructured interview.

Recognition of the importance of the above issues when developing and implementing the situational interview will ensure appropriate usage of this technique. By adhering to the steps outlined in this chapter and following the guidelines for question development and response scoring, interview panels will be more successful in selecting individuals who are capable of performing successfully on the job. Documenting of selection decisions and the bases upon which employees have been chosen will also be enhanced by the procedures described here and in the previous chapter.

References

Cascio, W.F. (1993), *Applied Psychology in Personnel Management*, (4th edn), Englewood Cliffs, NJ: Prentice-Hall.

Bem, D. (1972), 'Self-Perception Theory', in L. Berkowitz (ed.), *Advances in Social Psychology*, (6), New York: Academic Press.

Gabris, G.T. and Rock, S.M. (1991), 'Situational Interviews and Job-Performance: The Results in One Public Agency', *Public Personnel Management*, **20** (4), 469–83.

Gatewood, R.D. and Feild, H.S. (1990), *Human Resource Selection*, (2nd edn), Chicago: Dryden Press.

Latham, G.P. (1989), 'The Reliability, Validity and Practicality of the Situational Interview', in R.W. Eder and G.R. Ferris (eds), *The Employment Interview* , 169–82, Newbury Park, CA: Sage.

Latham, G.P.and Saari, L.M. (1984), 'Do People Do What They Say? Further Studies on the Situational Interview', *Journal of Applied Psychology*, **69**, 569–73.

Latham, G.P., Saari, L.M., Pursell, E.D. and Campion, M.A. (1980), 'The Situational Interview', *Journal of Applied Psychology*, **65**, 422–27.

Locke, E. (1968), 'Toward a Theory of Task Motivation and Incentives', *Organizational Behavior and Human Performance*, **4**, 157–89.

Maurer, S.D. and Fay, C. (1988), 'Effect of Situational Interviews, Conventional Structured Interviews, and Training on Interview Rating Agreement: An Experimental Analysis', *Personnel Psychology*, **41**, 329–44.

Motowidlo, S.J., Dunnette, M.D. and Carter, G.W. (1990), 'An Alternative Selection Procedure: The Low-Fidelity Simulation', *Journal of Applied Psychology*, **75**, 640–47.

Stohr-Gilmore, M.K., Stohr-Gilmore, M.W. and Kistler, N. (1990), 'Improving Selection Outcomes with the Use of Situational Interviews: Empirical Evidence from a Study of Correctional Officers for New Generation Jails', *Review of Public Personnel Administration*, **10** (2), 1–18.

Weekly, J.A. and Gier, J.A. (1987), 'Reliability and Validity of the Situational Interview for a Sales Position', *Journal of Applied Psychology*, **72**, 484–87.

6
IMPLEMENTING A STRUCTURED INTERVIEW APPROACH

In previous chapters we have discussed why and how to conduct the two principal types of structured employment interviews. Now we examine some of the finer details involved in implementing a structured approach. They include:

- opening and closing the structured interview;
- additional questions which can be included in a structured interview;
- using several interviewers;
- combining BDI and situational formats;
- short cuts in conducting structured interviews;
- structured interviews in relation to other selection methods; and
- implementing a structured interview approach throughout the organization.

OPENING AND CLOSING THE STRUCTURED INTERVIEW

Employment interviews should start with a friendly greeting. Job candidates are often nervous at an interview, and a warm welcome from the interviewer can help relax the candidate from the start. You might ask the candidate if she or he had any trouble finding your location, or mention that you were favourably impressed with the applicant's résumé/application form. Just as with structured interview questions themselves, avoid opening questions that are not job-related and that delve into the candidate's personal life (such as, '*How was your weekend?*').

Next explain the purpose and format of the interview, including:

○ that you will be asking about specific past experiences which relate to the requirements for the job (in the case of BDIs), or that you will be presenting a series of hypothetical job situations, asking the candidate for responses to them (in the case of situational interviews);

○ that you will be taking notes; and

○ when the candidate should ask any questions concerning the position and the organization.

Structured interviews are often arranged with interviewer questions first, and candidate questions toward the end of the interview. Candidates might still ask the occasional question about the position or organization earlier, but providing such a structure at the start of the interview lets candidates know that time has been reserved for their questions as well.

Keep the overview of the interview format simple, and avoid interview jargon when introducing the interview. For example, in the case of BDIs, say that you will be asking about specific experiences related to the job requirements, rather than saying either that you will be seeking 'behavioural descriptions', or that you will want to know about specific situations, their behaviour, and the outcome of that behaviour.

Before beginning structured questions, you might summarize and check your understanding of the candidate's relevant work experience. Such a summary refamiliarizes the interviewer with the candidate (often necessary when a number of interviews are conducted in a single day), and provides a common ground of understanding. It also can relax the candidate to start with short, general answers regarding his or her past experience (for example, '*Yes, I have been with Acme Electronics for the past three years*').

After opening the interview, you then begin the structured questions for each of the competencies. Questions which are likely to be easier to answer should be positioned early in the interview, and more difficult questions later. This strategy is less likely to threaten candidates' confidence than asking difficult questions first. Similarly, if a candidate in a BDI may not have experiences in a particular competency area, place questions related to that area toward the end of the behavioural description questions.

Before closing the interview, the candidate should be given time to ask questions, and if you took notes, review them to be sure that all questions were asked. In the case of BDIs, make sure that all behavioural descriptions are complete (situation, behaviour, outcome). To accomplish this, the interviewer might conclude the structured interview questions by asking the candidate to take a moment to think of any questions concerning the position or organization while the interviewer quickly reviews his or her notes.

In closing, it is customary to thank the candidate for the interview, and to explain what the next step in the interview process will be (a phone call or letter will be sent by a certain time, the scheduling of a second interview).

DEVELOPING RAPPORT THROUGHOUT THE INTERVIEW

Making the interview as relaxed as possible puts the candidate in the best position to remember and communicate his or her past experience, gives a favourable impression to the candidate (irrespective of whether the job is offered and accepted) and is common courtesy. In addition to smiling and offering a friendly greeting, compliment the candidate where appropriate, and show understanding for her or his experiences. You might arrange seating so that you are both at a table, sitting on two adjacent sides, rather than on opposite sides of a desk.

ADDITIONAL QUESTIONS WHICH CAN BE INCLUDED IN A STRUCTURED INTERVIEW

Virtually all questions in a BDI are designed to elicit behavioural descriptions from candidates, and in a situational interview to elicit responses to hypothetical job situations. There are two types of other questions, however, that are sometimes required. They are technical knowledge questions and willingness questions.

TECHNICAL KNOWLEDGE QUESTIONS

When particular technical knowledge has been identified as a competency required for a job, it can be tapped either through applicants' past experience (that is, behavioural descriptions) by asking for situations in which technical knowledge has been used, by asking situational questions concerning technical knowledge, or by asking questions to test that technical knowledge. If a large number of positions in a particular job are likely to be filled, questions concerning applicants' technical knowledge can be asked more reliably and cheaply by developing a paper-and-pencil (or computer-based) test.

WILLINGNESS QUESTIONS

Some jobs require that those appointed to them are willing to do certain things, like working particular shifts, travelling, being relocated, and working under certain physical work conditions. If candidates must be willing to do certain things once hired, the requirements are not considered 'competencies', and so candidates are not rated on them. Candidates are either willing or not willing to do them. However, any that are not absolute requirements (such as, the organization would only *prefer* someone who is willing to work certain shifts) may be rated, just as other competencies are.

USING SEVERAL INTERVIEWERS

Structured interviews often, but not always, involve several interviewers, either in the form of a panel or 'board' interview (a number of interviewers present at the same interview) or through sequential interviews, in which the candidate is interviewed two or more times, each with different interviewers. Despite the fact that two recent studies have questioned the assumption that several interviewers leads to improved validity (Searcy et al., 1993; Wiesner and Cronshaw, 1988), we believe that there are still advantages to using more than one interviewer in the BDI. If two interviewers are present in the interview, one can take notes while the other asks the questions. Interviewers can compare their ratings of candidates, which may provide a more reliable rating as well as a common base upon which to discuss differences in ratings.

Finally, interviews for complex jobs often involve many competencies. Two or more interviews, conducted sequentially by different staff, allows for a large number of competencies to be divided between interviewers. Competencies of the highest importance are typically covered in all interviews, while those of lesser importance are split between interviews.

It is not uncommon to have five or more interviewers on a panel for some positions, particularly professional and managerial jobs within public sector organizations. This practice seems less common in the private sector. Many private sector organizations use a line manager and a personnel specialist as an interview team when conducting BDIs in a panel, and involve higher-level managers for follow-up interviews with a short list of those given a first interview. Generally, having a greater number of interviewers on a panel may feel threatening to the candidate, particularly for low-level jobs, and therefore we recommend that panels be limited to two or three interviewers in most cases.

If a panel interview is used, roles of panel members must be clear before the interview. One panel member should lead the interview by providing the opening and closing, and there should be agreement about who asks what questions. Particular behavioural description questions should be asked of all candidates by the same panel member, to minimize differences across candidates in how the question is asked and how follow-up questions are used.

COMBINING BDI AND SITUATIONAL FORMATS

While BDIs and situational interview methods have been developed independently, we see no reason why they could not be used in combination, within the same interview, if both types of questions are warranted. For some jobs, interviewers may wish to consider a combination of candidates' past experiences and responses to hypothetical job situations. Such an approach might be useful when most applicants would be expected to have some, but not much relevant previous experience for a particular competency. A telecommunications company hiring customer service representatives might wish to assess candidates' previous service-related experiences, as well as how candidates would respond to a variety of hypothetical job situations.

A critical feature of situational interviews is the predetermined scoring key, and so if situational questions are to be asked, such a scoring key must be developed. When an interview includes both BDI and situational questions, scoring keys might be developed for *all* questions. In fact, rating candidates' responses to BDI questions is likely to be *enhanced* by using a scoring key similar to those developed for situational questions.

SHORT CUTS IN CONDUCTING STRUCTURED INTERVIEWS

Structured interviews take more time to implement than unstructured interviews, and so short cuts have been taken by some, particularly in the preparation phase of behavioural description interviews. In general, we do not recommend taking such short cuts because they are likely to erode the superior reliability, validity and fairness of structured interviews. Conclusions drawn from research about the effectiveness of structured interviews have been based on studies using procedures similar to those we have presented in this book. Therefore, the extent to which such short cuts affect interview outcomes is unknown, and is an area which might be addressed in future research.

The most common short cut we have seen taken with behavioural description interviews is in the derivation of competencies. Even when there are plenty of incumbents and supervisors, some organizations simply generate a list of competencies – sometimes from tasks, but frequently for the job as a whole. Firms selling behavioural description interview 'packages' often develop a list of competencies, from which someone familiar with the job selects those that are most important, usually through ratings. Software packages have been developed recently to facilitate such competency ratings, which generate lists of important competencies, suggested interview questions and, in some cases, complete interview schedules.

Even with such short cuts, these structured interviews are likely to be superior to unstructured approaches because questions are job-related and involve specific past experiences, and because interviews are still conducted and evaluated in a systematic way. There is no evidence to suggest that they will achieve the same high levels of reliability, validity and fairness which have been demonstrated for structured interviews developed from a thorough job analysis of the particular position.

If critical incidents are not developed in the job analysis phase, interview questions are job-related in only a *general* way. Identifying important competencies from the job as a whole, rather than from tasks, runs the risk of missing some important competencies or failing to weight competencies appropriately. Involving only one or two persons familiar with the job in identifying competencies fails to control for idiosyncratic biases of those SMEs. A behavioural description interview approach which involves only the rating of a set of competencies cannot really lay claim to the reliability, validity, and fairness demonstrated in structured interview research.

In sum, structured interviews with short cuts are probably better than unstructured approaches, but they are likely to be less reliable, valid and fair than the structured interviews approach we have outlined in Chapters 3–5.

STRUCTURED INTERVIEWS IN RELATION TO OTHER SELECTION METHODS

For most jobs, structured interviews are best used in conjunction with other means of collecting job-related information from applicants because they can either save time and expense, or provide information about candidates not readily available through the interview. In this section we will review other common selection methods, and discuss how they might be used in conjunction with structured interviews.

Two methods should be used in conjunction with structured interviews in virtually all situations: résumés or application forms and reference checks. Résumés (or curricula vitae) and application forms provide a basis for quickly and inexpensively short-listing applicants. Application forms are preferable when a large number of applicants are anticipated, warranting the time it takes to develop them.

RÉSUMÉS AND APPLICATION BLANKS

Résumés and application blanks are most suited for determining whether applicants possess minimum requirements for a job, such as qualifications, licences, and minimum levels of work experience. The reviewer need only check to see whether or not the candidate meets the minimum requirement.

For many jobs, however, simply screening for minimum job requirements fails to reduce the applicant pool to a manageable short list for interviewing. In such cases, subjective judgements are usually made about each candidate, based on what is presented in the résumé or application form. Whenever subjective judgements are made, systematic processes for identifying competencies and rating candidates should be employed, just as we have discussed in previous chapters for structured interviews.

From the list of competency requirements developed in the job analysis, those that can be assessed through résumés or application forms should be identified. These competencies should be critical to job success and be assessable on paper. For example, assume that financial analysis is an important competency requirement for a particular job, and that virtually everyone who possesses skills in this area will have acquired them based on particular work experiences. While financial analysis skills are not *directly* assessable through candidates' résumés, they are *indirectly* assessable through checking for relevant work experiences.

Just as a number of interviewers are used in structured interviews to reduce idiosyncratic bias, so should a number of raters be used to review and score competencies on résumés or application blanks in cases where the possession of particular competencies is not clearly 'yes' or 'no'. Two or three people should independently review résumés or application forms, scoring relevant competencies, using a scoring key similar to those presented for structured interviews (*see* Chapter 4 and Part II H and I).

REFERENCES

Reference checks also provide information which complements that obtained through structured interviews. Both reference checks and letters of recommendation are often referred to as 'references', but reference checks are far more valuable. Letters of recommendation suffer from being global and virtually all positive, thus providing a poor basis on which to differentiate candidates. Reference checks, on the other hand, can be focused on specific job competencies and can be used to elicit both positive and negative work experiences of candidates.

Choose the most critical competencies for the reference check, even if those competencies have been covered in the structured interview. In this way, the reference check serves as a second source of information for ratings of important job requirements. Additionally, many interviewers use references as a means to check for any unusual, potentially problematic aspects of candidates (such as, dishonesty, tardiness, absenteeism, theft). The absence of such characteristics may not have been identified as critical competencies for the job. While these characteristics are important for most jobs, they are often not included in a list of competencies assessed in structured interviews because they are likely to occur with a minority of candidates, and candidates with problems in these areas may not disclose them in an interview.

When used with behaviour description interviews, reference checks should occur *after* candidates have been interviewed, to follow up on descriptions of experiences which have been provided in the interview. (They can be conducted either before or after situational interviews.) While they can be conducted either verbally (usually over the telephone) or through a written form, referees may be more honest about negative information if it is acquired verbally, and not in-writing. Finally, reference checks should be sent to candidates' recent supervisors, if possible, because they are typically most familiar with candidates' past work experiences.

Many candidates are reluctant to let their employer know they are applying for other jobs, making it difficult to seek information from current supervisors (which is all the more reason to use reference checks as a last step in the selection process). Some employing organizations *insist upon* the inclusion of a reference from the current supervisor, while others are willing to forgo it. In some cases, the reference check with the current supervisor may be postponed until a tentative selection decision has been made, so that the reference check with the current supervisor is used only as a final check. This tactic is less advantageous than using the current supervisor reference as a *basis* of selecting the preferred candidate to begin with, but it may be better than not involving the current supervisor at all.

In deciding which of these approaches to employ, consider the quality of the candidates' other references and, based on all other information, how close the candidate's performance in the selection system has been to that of other candidates. If a candidate has provided other referees who are familiar with the candidate's recent work, or if the candidate has been judged far superior than other candidates in other aspects of the selection system, there may be less need to hear from the current supervisor.

Information can be obtained from referees in the form of either narrative descriptions of candidate's previous work, competency ratings, or both. Narrative descriptions should be sought in a similar format to that which is used in behavioural description interviews; they should be asked for specific examples of the candidate's past performance in relation to predetermined competencies, and each description should include the situation faced, what the candidate did, and the outcome.

> *Example:* Project planning is one of the critical requirements of the job Chris has applied for. Has Chris done project planning when she worked with you? Can you tell me about a recent project plan she has developed?

Additionally, the reference check should also be used to follow up on critical behavioural descriptions provided by the candidate, confirming the situation, the candidate's behaviour, and the outcome.

If asked to provide a summary evaluation of candidates on specific competencies, referees should be asked about the extent of their experience with candidates, giving more weight to information provided by referees with the most experience of candidates.

While interviews, résumés/application forms and reference checks are used as sources of applicant information for filling virtually all jobs, other selection methods may be used for particular kinds of jobs. These include personality tests, cognitive ability tests, tests of specific abilities, work samples, and simulations. Most of these methods can be effectively used in combination with structured interviews.

PERSONALITY TESTS

Personality tests have been used frequently in personnel selection, particularly for managerial and sales positions. The predictive validity of these tests has traditionally been weak, for several reasons. First, most tests in use were not developed specifically for organizational settings, and so most traits, as well as questions associated with those traits, were not job-related, analogous to asking candidates questions in interviews about areas unrelated to job performance.

Second, there has been a problem of test-takers 'faking good'. Candidates know the type of job they are applying for, and can guess how to respond in a personality test to maximize their chances of being offered a job. When asked on a personality inventory which she or he would like most to do on a Friday evening, go to a party or read a book, the candidate for a sales position is likely to (correctly) infer that the 'go to a party' answer is more likely to get her or him the job offer. Psychologists have attempted to make personality test questions less transparent to test-takers, but with little success; generally, the more oblique the question, the less its validity.

Finally, most personality tests are designed to tap many (ten or more) personality dimensions (or traits), and those interpreting test scores assess candidates far too frequently on their entire personality test profile, rather than only on dimensions identified via a thorough job analysis.

Recently, the identification of job-specific personality characteristics have been developed, and when linked to specific jobs through job analysis, higher (though only moderate) predictive validities have been found (Tett, Jackson and Rothstein, 1991). Such tests still have limited application in an organization using structured interviews, because job-related dimensions tapped with personality tests (such as, conscientiousness, agreeableness) are very similar to those which can be covered in structured interviews, and so, little additional information is gained through the personality tests. However, other traits identified in job-related personality tests, such as emotional stability and extroversion, differ from typical competencies used in structured interviews, suggesting that some personality tests *may* have a role to play in a selection system using structured interviews. It has been our experience that, for most jobs, personality tests do not offer sufficient information beyond what can be obtained in a structured interview to justify the expense of using them.

COGNITIVE ABILITY TESTS

Many jobs are cognitively complex, that is they require analytical thinking, decision making, and ability to learn on the part of the job holder. Examples of such jobs include most managerial positions, technical analysts, computer programmers, and troubleshooters. Recent research which has spanned hundreds of validation studies on cognitive ability tests has indicated that they are quite valid in predicting job success for such jobs. This research has also drawn a few other relevant conclusions regarding these tests.

First, minority group members can be expected to score significantly below majority group members on these tests, running the risk of reducing the number of minority group members hired if cognitive ability tests are the primary selection method. This research has concentrated primarily on comparisons of blacks' and whites' test scores in the USA, but similar effects may exist for other cultural minorities. Consequently, these tests should be used cautiously, and in conjunction with other selection methods less prone to adverse impact on cultural minorities, such as structured employment interviews.

Second, the validity of long, multifaceted cognitive ability tests seems no greater than for shorter, general cognitive tests. There appears to be no benefit of administering lengthy multiple aptitude batteries over their simpler test counterparts.

Third, cognitive ability tests seem to predict *early* performance in a job better than *long-term* performance. Cognitively complex jobs appear to require the most cognitive ability of job holders when new to the job. Once enough time has passed for job holders to get a good grasp of the job (perhaps a year or so after being hired), cognitive ability has less influence on job performance. Consequently, these tests may have a minimal contribution to make in the selection of staff who are expected to have a relatively long tenure in jobs which are expected to change little over time.

Most cognitive ability tests must be administered by a qualified psychologist, which should be taken into account when estimating the costs of testing candidates. There are, however, tests which have been developed recently which can be administered by non-psychologists, provided they have attended courses provided by the test vendor.

For cognitively complex jobs, structured interviews and cognitive ability tests can be used well together, using the test to tap the cognitive facets of the job, and focusing the interview on other competencies. The incremental advantage of adding a cognitive ability test to a selection system which includes a structured interview is a function of the extent to which each tap different underlying competencies. While there is likely to be no more than moderate overlap between cognitive ability tests and BDIs, in the case of the situational interview, there may be substantial overlap. Campion, Pursell and Brown (1988) have suggested the possibility that situational interview scores may be based largely on cognitive ability – persons with greater cognitive ability simply intuit better the 'right' answers. More research is needed to test whether this is true, and if it is, either a cognitive ability test or a situational interview used *alone* is about as effective as both used together.

TESTS OF SPECIFIC ABILITIES

Valid tests have been developed to measure abilities other than cognitive ability as well, such as physical, mechanical, programming and typing, to name a few. They often reveal the level of performance a candidate is capable of far better than can be gleaned from answers in an interview. For example, results of a typing test yield more reliable information on typing speed and accuracy than can be determined in an interview.

These tests can be used effectively in combination with structured interviews. Once the job analysis has been completed, and an ability has been identified which might be assessed through testing, possible tests should be explored. Many tests of job-related abilities can be administered by persons without specific qualifications, and leads for finding them can often be obtained from one's local association of personnel managers.

WORK SAMPLES

Some competencies can best be demonstrated through samples of candidates' work. A direct evaluation of such work is usually more effective than simply talking about the work in a structured interview. When reviewing the list of competencies developed in the job analysis, identify any which could be assessed through a direct evaluation of candidates' previous work (examples of previously written reports, correspondence, repair work, programming, art work, and so on). In many cases, candidates can be asked to bring samples of their work to the interview.

SIMULATIONS

Job candidates can be asked to participate in a simulation of the job being applied for, in which their behaviour is scored according to a set of competencies or dimensions. Many aspects of jobs have been simulated, such as operating machinery, individual and team assembly operations, and doctor–patient interactions.

In simulations, candidates actually work, much like they would on the job, while being observed by trained assessors. How assessors rate, discuss, and make final decisions about candidates' appropriateness for jobs is quite similar to the rating and decision-making procedures we have discussed previously in the context of structured interviews.

Probably the most common simulations in personnel selection have been those associated with assessment centres. Assessment centres can be used to assess interpersonal and administrative skills, and are often used for managerial positions. Assessment centres usually take between one and two days, and contain a series of exercises (such as in-baskets, leaderless group discussions, simulated presentations) along with paper-and-pencil tests. Most of the competencies/dimensions assessed through exercises are similar to those tapped by structured interviews.

Predictive validities for assessment centres have been similar to those found for structured interviews, however, their implementation costs are much higher. Typically, there is only a 2:1 or 3:1 ratio between candidates and assessors, which, over the course of a two-day assessment, adds up to a substantial expense per candidate. Since both assessment centres and structured interviews tap similar competencies, and because of the high cost of conducting assessment centres, there is questionable value in conducting an assessment centre in addition to, or instead of, structured interviews. Many organizations, however, conduct assessment centres – both with and without structured interviews, and believe that the candidate information they receive outweighs the cost of the assessment centre.

IMPLEMENTING STRUCTURED INTERVIEWS THROUGHOUT THE ORGANIZATION

Given the superiority of structured interviews over unstructured ones, it is sensible to use structured interviewing as the standard operating procedure throughout the organization. Jobs for which many candidates will be interviewed can be targeted for situational interviews, while BDIs can be developed for other jobs for which there might be fewer applicants.

Situational interviews are typically developed by personnel specialists or industrial/organizational psychologists, in conjunction with people familiar with the target job. Behaviour description interviewing, on the other hand, can be taught to line managers and personnel specialists so that it can be used as needed, with or without supervision from the human resources/personnel department. To be effective, training should provide written descriptions and necessary forms to be used to prepare for interviews after training.

Behaviour modelling has been found to be a particularly effective approach for teaching complex interpersonal skills (Burke and Day, 1986), such as how to conduct structured interviews. Behaviour modelling training is based on social learning theory (Bandura, 1971; 1977), and involves:

○ providing a description of the skills to be learned;
○ showing one or more positive models of the target interaction (for example, a video simulation of a manager conducting a structured interview);
○ giving trainees an opportunity to practice and receive feedback on their use of the newly learned skills; and

○ emphasizing the transfer of skills to the workplace, through providing written summaries of steps and other tools, as well as arranging
for trainees' managers to support their using newly learned skills.

Training in BDIs can be purchased as a package from a training vendor,
or developed internally. Firms which sell BDI training typically advertise
in practitioner-oriented personnel and training journals, such as
Personnel, Personnel Administrator, Training and Development Journal,
and *Training* magazine. In evaluating packaged BDI training programmes, consider how consistent the skills in the programme are with
the BDI steps we have described in Chapters 3 and 4. Short cuts in the
procedure are likely to result in poorer reliability, validity, and fairness, as
we have discussed earlier. Also, consider the quality of the materials provided, including videos.

Developing a programme internally can be cost-effective for large organizations, provided necessary resources are available or can be contracted
(course developers, printing and videotaping facilities and so on).
Guidelines for developing behaviour modelling training programmes can
be found in Decker and Nathan (1985) and Robinson (1982).

CONCLUSION

In this book we have described two methods for conducting structure
employment interviews. These two techniques – behavioural description
interviewing and situational interviewing – have been shown by
researchers to be both reliable and valid in selecting job applicants. If the
steps we have described are followed carefully and systematically, the
procedures outlined here will improve the selection process, and therefore result in more effective hiring of personnel.

In today's economic environment, selection of high-performance
employees is becoming an increasingly important area of human resource
management. Making the right choices at 'the front end' will ensure that
performance problems on the job are minimized and that there is a good
match between employee skills and competencies and organizational
expectations. Employment interviews form a major element of the selection process and typically make a substantial contribution to decisions
about whom to hire. Unfortunately, however, past approaches have not
always been optimal, often leading to haphazard and ill-formed judgements about job candidates.

Behavioural description and situational interviews represent alternative
approaches which, if used properly, can have a significant impact on

selection processes and outcomes. Structured interviews usually take a little more time and effort to develop, but the benefits which they offer make the investment of this time and energy worth while, and will enhance individual job performance and organizational productivity.

References

Bandura, A. (1971), *Psychological Modeling*, New York: Lieber-Atherton.

Bandura, A. (1977), *Social Learning Theory*, Englewood Cliffs, NJ: Prentice Hall.

Burke, M.J. and Day, R.R. (1986), 'A Cumulative Study of the Effectiveness of Managerial Training', *Journal of Applied Psychology*, **71**, 232–45.

Campion, M.A., Pursell, E.D. and Brown, B.K. (1988), 'Structured Interviewing: Raising the Psychometric Properties of the Employment Interview', *Personnel Psychology*, **42**, 1–24.

Decker, P.J. and Nathan, B.R. (1985), *Behavior Modeling Training*, New York: Praeger.

Robinson, J.C. (1982), *Developing Managers Through Behavior Modeling*, Austin, TX: Learning Concepts.

Searcy, C.A., Woods, P.N., Gatewood, R. and Lance, C. (1993), 'The Validity of Structured Interviews: A Meta-Analytic Search for Moderators'. Paper presented at the Society of Industrial Psychologists 1993 Annual Meeting, San Francisco, CA.

Tett, R.P., Jackson, D.N. and Rothstein, M. (1991), 'Personality Measures as Predictors of Job Performance: A Meta-Analytic Review', *Personnel Psychology*, **44**, 703–42.

Wiesner, W.H. and Cronshaw, S.F. (1988), 'A Meta-Analytic Investigation of the Impact of Interview Format and Degree of Structure on the Validity of the Employment Interview', *Journal of Occupational Psychology*, **61**, 275–90.

PART II

❖

A

SAMPLE QUESTIONNAIRE TO GENERATE CRITICAL INCIDENTS

*Note that this questionnaire has been designed to elicit critical incidents for the job **as a whole**. Alternatively, the questionnaire could be designed to seek critical incidents from each respondent for each main job task.*

The purpose of this questionnaire is to identify examples of particularly effective or ineffective performance for the job of *Production Supervisor*, which will be used to develop employment interview questions.

Please think of three incidents in which a production supervisor has performed particularly effectively, and three involving ineffective performance.

These must be incidents that have actually occurred and with which you are familiar. Please maintain anonymity by referring to the persons involved in the incidents by title only (not by name).

For each incident, please include: (a) the situation that the production supervisor faced; (b) what, specifically, the supervisor did; and (c) the outcome of the supervisor's behaviour.

Here is an example of a critical incident, for a different kind of job (technician):

Situation faced: The technician was approached by a co-worker to help retrieve a lost data file, a task which is not within the incumbent's regular duties.

What the technician did: The technician responded by saying that the co-worker should have maintained a backup file, that it 'served her right', and that retrieving others' lost data files was not part of his responsibility.

The outcome of the technician's behaviour: The co-worker was unable to finish her report when it was due, and did not approach the incumbent for help again.

Now please describe three critical incidents of effective behaviour and three of ineffective behaviour for the job of Production Supervisor.

Effective incident 1

Situation faced:

What production supervisor did:

Outcome of production supervisor's behaviour:

Effective incident 2

Situation faced:

What production supervisor did:

Outcome of production supervisor's behaviour:

Effective incident 3

Situation faced:

What production supervisor did:

Outcome of production supervisor's behaviour:

B
COMPETENCIES COMMON TO MANY JOBS

Analytic thinking: Identifies concerns and causes of problems and finds links between information from various sources.

Achievement orientation: Demonstrates motivation to achieve results; perseveres with plans.

Conscientiousness: Works steadily, efficiently and dependably; checks work thoroughly for errors/omissions.

Creativity: Develops innovative solutions to work-related problems; identifies potential opportunities and ways to capitalize on them.

Customer service orientation: Is courteous, patient, pleasant, and helpful with customers; shows understanding for customers' concerns; takes actions to accommodate customer needs whenever possible.

Decision making: Identifies a variety of alternatives before selecting a course of action, weighs advantages and disadvantages of each alternative, and chooses a logical course of action based on available information and reasonable assumptions.

Delegating: Considers job responsibilities, workloads, skills, and developmental needs in effectively allocating work among staff. Communicates specific work expectations while delegating tasks, discusses ways of accomplishing tasks, and follows up to ensure successful task completion.

Flexibility: Adapts approach to fit with changing conditions, tasks, responsibilities, or people.

High work standards: Establishes high goals for self and others; seeks challenging assignments; sets high standard for own work performance; works steadily and conscientiously without wasting time.

Initiative: Takes actions to achieve favourable outcomes for the organization, beyond minimum performance expectations, and seeks opportunities to improve work procedures.

Keeping informed: Maintains an awareness of events and changes inside and outside of the organization, as well as advances in own job area or profession.

Relations with others: Is pleasant, cooperative, and gets along well with others. Keeps manager informed, reports problems promptly, and seeks guidance when needed. Develops and maintains a network of personal contacts within the organization.

People management: Enlists support, cooperation and participation when influencing and guiding others toward the accomplishment of tasks. Monitors performance on an ongoing basis, providing positive feedback for effective performance, and coaching to resolve performance difficulties.
(Note that this competency can apply to a position with managerial responsibility as well as a position in which the incumbent has no direct control over others' work, such as in a project leader position.)

Planning: Plans actions to accomplish goals systematically, including establishing time-frames, allocating resources, and following up on details.

Self-confidence: Asserts own point of view, even when it differs from others (e.g., manager's); shows confidence in own skills and capacity to complete tasks; seeks necessary resources for self and/or staff to work effectively.

Sensitivity: Demonstrates an awareness of others' concerns, interests and positions, and takes into consideration the impact that decisions and plans are likely to have on them.

Stability: Performs stably while under pressure or in a changing work environment.

Technical skill/knowledge: Demonstrates sufficient level of understanding and skill in required technical area. (The specific content of this dimension needs to be defined for each job.)

Written communication: Expresses ideas in writing clearly, with correct grammar and spelling, and in a well-organized way.

Verbal communication: Expresses ideas orally with clarity, appropriate grammar, pace and non-verbal gestures; listens effectively.

Note: We have developed this list from competencies we have seen used most frequently in our experience with organizations who have developed structured interviews and from the sources listed below:

Gatewood R.D. and Feild, H.S. (1990), *Human Resource Selection,* (2nd edn), Chicago: Dryden Press.

Janz, T., Hellervik, L. and Gilmore, D.C. (1986), *Behavioral Description Interviewing,* Boston: Allyn & Bacon.

Thornton, G.C., III, and Byham, W.C. (1982), *Assessment Centers and Managerial Performance,* New York: Academic Press.

Woodruffe, C. (1990), *Assessment Centres: Identifying and Developing Competence,* London: Institute of Personnel Management.

C

EXAMPLE OF JOB-SPECIFIC COMPETENCY DEFINITIONS WITH CRITICAL INCIDENTS

Position: Hospital Charge Nurse

Competencies

People management: Enlists support, cooperation and participation when influencing and guiding others toward the accomplishment of tasks. Negotiates with patients, staff, peers, doctors and senior management in order to achieve the optimal outcome for all concerned. Monitors performance on an ongoing basis, providing positive feedback for effective performance and coaches to resolve performance difficulties. Acts as an advocate for staff.

Critical incident A

Situation   Just before Christmas, two of the nurses that worked in this particular ward had deaths in their family. They could not come to work, therefore the ward had two staff members short and the safety of the unit was compromised.

Behaviour   The Charge Nurse negotiated with other staff members to do extra duties, which was particularly difficult because the duties were night shifts. She made out a list of people whom she could contact, making sure that those individuals would not have a terrible roster by having to do an extra night duty. She also made sure that these individuals were not the same ones that she had asked recently. She rang them up and told them the facts, and that the roster needed to be changed around to cover the night duty so that the unit was safe and that the nurses who were on duty that night would have sufficient help. The Charge Nurse made sure that she asked the nurses in a way that did not put any pressure on them to say yes. She accepted if they said no, and mentioned to them that there were other choices.

Outcome   Staff voluntarily worked those extra night duties that were needed. Safety needs were met.

Critical incident B

Situation   A night nurse in the ward had been upsetting patients verbally and this had been going on for some time. The patients in the morning would complain, and comments were received from the other nurses that the patients were upset, and that they were frightened by the nurse.

Behaviour   The Charge Nurse brought the concerned nurse in and talked to him. He did not realize that there was anything wrong. This individual's manner was very harsh, because he has had a lot of problems at home, but he said that he was going to work on improving his performance and that he would seek more counselling on his personal life. Things improved for about 12 weeks and then slipped again. One morning three patients made complaints about specific things that this individual had done. The Charge Nurse wrote them all down, rang the human resources manager, and lodged a disciplinary complaint with the union representative. A meeting was held with all the parties involved, and negotiations were made.

Outcome   The staff member came off night shifts. While he was upset about this, because of the money involved, he remained to work on day shifts and became a different person. He improved to being a wonderful nurse, and even spoke to the Charge Nurse and thanked her for taking the disciplinary action. He felt much happier now because he was not stressed out and he was able to increase his hours so that he would receive the same amount of money as previously.

Initiative: Realizes the need for change and seeks feasible solutions. Takes actions to achieve favourable outcomes for the organization, beyond minimum performance expectations, and seeks opportunities to improve work procedures.

Critical incident A

Situation   A new medical consultant joined a ward. There was a shortage of beds in that ward, therefore negotiations were made to use beds in another ward, to accommodate the minor cases which this new consultant would be dealing with. This other ward came under a different service area, therefore did not have sufficient knowledge of the type of patients who were going to be admitted as a result of the new consultant working on their premises.

Behaviour   The Charge Nurse, together with a clinical resource nurse, wrote up an information booklet specifying the types of medical conditions which would be referred to that ward, and set up in-service education sessions where they would educate staff on a weekly basis for a period of 12 weeks.

Outcome   The patients that had been sent to that ward had minimal complications. Staff were keen to receive patients, not just the more minor cases, and felt that they had sufficient basic skills to look after this type of patient. They were happy to liaise with the ward.

Critical incident B

Situation   A Charge Nurse realized that his ward did not have a lot of information about the work the nurses did and what the patients were like. He had wanted to introduce a patient data sheet for staff to complete but felt that they would be resistant to the idea if not enough effort was put to it, because it would be considered just another type of documentation for nurses.

Behaviour   The Charge Nurse started introducing the idea quietly to the nurses, saying that this was something that was of interest, without pressing the issue any further. When the staff became more familiar with the idea, the Charge Nurse designed the data sheet, and then had a staff meeting so that it could be showed to them. He told them why he wanted it and how the information would help them. The Charge Nurse used the data sheet himself for the first three months so that any difficulties could be ironed out, and any ambiguous areas could be modified. After three months, another staff meeting was held and the Charge Nurse told the nurses that he would like them to try to complete the data sheets. Again, they were informed about the reasons for doing so and what benefits there were.

Outcome   There was some grumbling from staff saying that completing the forms was more work, but they were all willing to give it a go. Because the data sheet provided information on the type of work staff did, and statistics on the amount of nurses that were required to look after the patients, it ensured that the ward was sufficiently staffed. The information also indicated the types of patients which were treated, and staff felt that they could justify with hard evidence that there was a high level of tension and stress on their job. As a result, nurses were very pleased to be able to see what they had done every month, and how successful they had been.

Patient care: Ensures patient safety and provision of high-quality patient care, shows concern for the patient and their family, and provides help and support for them and any decisions that they make.

Critical incident A

Situation   A young woman was diabetic and the ward had grown to know her and her family very well. She was admitted to the ward more often within the last year but no one knew what was wrong with her. Finally, she was diagnosed as having a brain tumour as well as having diabetes.

Behaviour   The Charge Nurse went through all the grief with the parents. Doctors were very keen on giving the patient radiotherapy but she refused and said that she wanted to die with dignity. The Charge Nurse supported her and her family with that and set up a room with beds and lazyboys so when the patient's sister and sister-in-law came from Australia, she had them and the rest of her family with her all the time. They played music and they massaged, and stayed with her overnight. The Charge Nurse, together with the ward, supported everything they did. Staff were available but they let the family care for her.

Outcome   The family were appreciative of the support they received and the patient died quietly one night in the arms of her sister. A big difference was made to the feelings of the family because the Charge Nurse could have insisted on the advice of the doctors that she needed radiotherapy. By letting the patient die the way she wanted to, the family took with them good memories of how she had been treated.

Critical incident B

Situation   A nurse informed the Charge Nurse that the night before, a young patient's father came in and he was very upset and angry about everything that was going on with the son and his progress, and about what he was being told.

Behaviour   The Charge Nurse had never met this man before because he could only come up at night due to his work, but she knew the patient's mother really well. So the Charge Nurse thought it was best to talk to her informally, to see what the situation was. When the mother came in the next day, the Charge Nurse kept the conversation quite casual and just talked to her about her son, and asked her how she was feeling about everything, whether she felt that she was being kept informed. She was quite positive, and then the Charge Nurse mentioned that her husband had been up the night before and that he had been quite upset. The Charge Nurse offered to talk to him so that staff could give him any help or advice or whatever that he wanted, to help him understand things and feel better about the whole process.

Outcome   Although the patient's father did not want to take up that offer, he said that he was feeling better about everything, and he explained that when he interrupted that night, he was just letting off steam because it was a very stressful situation. He said he was, in fact, very happy about everything that went on, and the Charge Nurse made sure that he felt that way.

Open communication: Develops and maintains open communication channels with all staff. Distributes and interprets (when necessary) information from, and decisions by, senior management.

Critical incident A

Situation   Management was passing a lot of information through charge nurses to staff. Most of this information was presented in newsletters, though some was conveyed in memos from senior management meetings. A Charge Nurse realized that staff were tired at the end of the day, and did not want to sit down and read lots of memos and newsletters.

Behaviour   Instead of presenting all the information, the Charge Nurse read the material once, then the second time round, she would highlight all the different points in various colours so it would look more interesting. She would also inform staff on any other information presented at meetings.

Outcome   They were able to look at highlighted pieces of information and were able to digest it. Hearing issues from their Charge Nurse made them feel more part of the whole organization.

Critical incident B

Situation   Nurses had traditionally worked with a piece of paper in their pocket, on which they would write down who their patients were for the day, and what type of treatments were required. From these notes they would construct their nursing care plan, according to patient needs. A consultancy firm came in and required all staff to fill in schedules.

Behaviour   The Charge Nurse worked through various types of schedules with her staff but felt that none of them were suitable. So she said to them: 'Okay, tell me what you want and we will come up with a schedule ourselves.' So between the Charge Nurse and a number of nurses, they worked out a schedule. It had to be abbreviated, so a grid was designed. The Charge Nurse typed and printed it out for use. It was used for a week and it worked well, fulfilling the criteria needed for staffing schedules. The Charge Nurse took it back to the next meeting with the consultancy firm, and told them: 'This is what we have developed, it's what my nurses are happy with. These are the reasons why they are happy with them. If we are to continue doing the schedules, we'll use this form, but we will continue to improve it.' The Charge Nurse persisted until she got the results that she had wanted.

Outcome   All departments started using the schedules. Although staff did not want them, they were more happy with them because they had developed them themselves. They felt that their Charge Nurse acted on behalf of them, instead of blindly accepting something that management wanted, but which they did not want.

Staff selection and development: Assesses technical and interpersonal fit of applicants in selection interviews, facilitates the integration of new staff, and shows commitment to employee development.

Critical incident A

Situation   A new medical consultant joined a particular ward.

Behaviour   The Charge Nurse facilitated the integration of the new medical consultant with the two other consultants who were working there, by making sure that she would speak out in meetings with the consultants. The Charge Nurse also facilitated integration with the nursing staff. She sat down with the new consultant and asked, 'I need to know what your expectations of the nurses are', and as she had listed those, the Charge Nurse then said, 'Well, what we do in that situation is . . .' and worked to achieve a mutual expectation of how things operated.

Outcome   After a period of about six weeks, the new consultant participated and contributed comfortably to group meetings. The three medical consultants became a very cohesive team. The new consultant also had faith that the nurses were going to do things the way he expected them to do, and nurses also knew what his expectations were and did not have to constantly second guess.

Critical incident B

Situation   A Charge Nurse conducted an interview for the position of junior staff nurse. The applicant and the Charge Nurse knew each other personally.

Behaviour   The Charge Nurse insisted on hiring that person despite advice from the nursing advisers about how they judged the person in the interview.

Outcome   The staff nurse was hired and he was a poor performer.

Planning and organization: Establishes courses of action to accomplish goals, including establishing time-frames and allocating resources. Demonstrates fairness in designing rosters, makes assessments of workloads and allocates staff accordingly.

Critical incident A

Situation   The Charge Nurse needed to make a roster for his staff and himself.

Behaviour   Instead of considering that a Charge Nurse's role is primarily managerial and that he only needed to be around between 8 a.m. and 5 p.m., from time to time he would do a night shift or an afternoon shift. He realized that health is a 24-hour service so it is important to work around the clock.

Outcome   The Charge Nurse could make a direct assessment of the sorts of issues that were facing his staff. This allowed him to make decisions as to how he should plan workloads and allocate staff and rostering. He gained credibility from staff because they knew that their Charge Nurse had actually seen the issues regularly firsthand.

Critical incident B

Situation   A Charge Nurse was asked to prepare a report to support her request for more resources (equipment) for her department. She needed to have it prepared in a week's time for it to be considered in the resource allocation process. Two days prior to the deadline, she was asked how she was getting on.

Behaviour   She said that she had not done it yet, but was collecting the information and that the proposal would meet the deadline. The day before her submission was due she was again approached, and once more said that she would meet the deadline. When the deadline came, the report was not completed and in fact she did not even have the information necessary to prepare it.

Outcome   The resources that she wanted and probably did need and could have justified were not forthcoming. In the struggle for resources, her case was completely dismissed because it was very inadequately made. The resources went elsewhere and staff in that department did not receive the equipment they needed.

D
SAMPLE FORM FOR REFINING AND RATING JOB TASKS

❖

Such a form could be completed by subject-matter experts (SMEs), such as managers of the job, persons holding the job, and others who are familiar with it, in order to refine a list of job tasks, from which competencies can later be inferred. The initial list of tasks that is used for this form should be developed from existing job descriptions and an interview with the person to whom the position reports.

In this particular example, the job of 'Project Leader, Performance Management System' is a newly created job, and so the initial list of tasks here represent what might have been developed by the Manager of Human Resource Planning and the General Manager. The reporting relationships and position objective have been included to provide background for those who would complete the form. Note that, because this is a new position, only the importance of tasks is rated here, rather than both importance and frequency.

The following tasks have been identified for the job of *'Project Leader, Performance Management System (PMS)'*, a temporary internal appointment.

Reporting relationships

The Project Leader will report to the Manager of Human Resource Planning. However, s/he will liaise closely with the general management team.

Objective

Various performance appraisal systems have been used through the region in the past, and general management has decided that a single consistent performance management/appraisal system (referred to as the Performance Management System – PMS) needs to be developed.

The project leader will lead a project team of approximately five members of the organization, representing various geographic and functional areas of the organization. This team will be responsible for developing, implementing and evaluating the new PMS.

Please read through the list and:

○ Add any tasks that you believe to be a part of this job which are not already included.
○ Place a line through any tasks that you believe are not part of this job.
○ Rate how important each task is to meeting the position objective on the following scale:

     1 – critically important
     2 – very important
     3 – somewhat important
     4 – nice to have, but not really important
     5 – not at all related to job success

Importance rating	*Tasks/responsibilities*
—	1. Provide input on the choice of project team members.
—	2. Maximize commitment to the PMS, ensure a high level of involvement of relevant constituencies within the organization, such as various levels of line and staff management, employees, and unions.
—	3. Lead team meetings.
—	4. Apply project management principles to ensure that tasks are accomplished and deadlines are met.
—	5. Keep the general management informed of progress through regular written reports and oral presentations.
—	6. Make oral presentations on the PMS to various groups within the organization.
—	7. (other) _____
—	8. (other) _____

E

SAMPLE FORM FOR INFERRING COMPETENCY REQUIREMENTS FROM JOB TASKS

To be used as a basis of seeking competency requirements from subject-matter experts (SMEs), through either interviews or surveys.

For the position of Project Leader, PMS, please list what you believe to be competencies (knowledge, skills, abilities) critical to the successful completion of each of the following six tasks/responsibilities.

A job description and list of competencies common to many jobs are attached.

Task/responsibility	*Competencies required*
1. Provide input on the choice of project team members.	_____
2. Maximize commitment to the PMS, ensure a high level of involvement of relevant constituencies within the organization, such as various levels of line and staff management, employees, and unions.	_____

Task/responsibility   *Competencies required*

3. Lead team meetings.   _____

                                                         _____

                                                         _____

                                                         _____

4. Apply project management principles to   _____
   ensure that tasks are accomplished and deadlines are met.   _____

                                                         _____

                                                         _____

5. Keep the general management informed of   _____
   progress through regular written reports and
   oral presentations.   _____

                                                         _____

                                                         _____

6. Make oral presentations on the PMS to vari-   _____
   ous groups within the organization.
                                                         _____

                                                         _____

                                                         _____

F
EXAMPLES OF BDI QUESTIONS FOR COMMON JOB COMPETENCIES

❖

The questions listed below are designed to elicit descriptions of *situations* faced by the candidate. In some cases, however, we have also included follow-up questions which may be asked about the candidate's behaviour and the outcome of the situation.

For example, the first question under *Analytic thinking* is 'Can you think of a recent situation you faced which required analytic thinking on your part?' Assuming the candidate says 'yes', the first follow-up questions should ask for background on the situation, the next would focus on what analysis the candidate did, and final questions would deal with the outcome(s) of that analysis.

This section is meant only as a guide. Two or three behavioural descriptions are usually sought for each competency, and so not all questions listed under each competency would be asked. Furthermore, the list is by no means exhaustive. Most jobs are likely to include some competencies which are not listed here, and there are several other questions that could be used to tap the competencies which are listed. The questions themselves are italicized; instructions to the interviewer are not in italics.

Questions are worded rather generically, and should be refined for specific jobs and candidates. For example, most questions have been written for candidates who are presently working in a related position, and they focus on experiences in the candidate's present position. Therefore questions should be reworded for persons who are not presently working, for persons who have not worked in organizations recently (or at all), for those who have been working in quite unrelated jobs and to focus on a candidate's particular experiences in previous jobs.

For recent college/university graduates, questions might be reworded to target aspects of their course work or extracurricular activities. Similarly, questions should be adapted for people who have not been working outside the home.

We have noted where competencies can also be assessed through other means, such as reference checks or behaviour in the interview itself.

Analytic thinking: Identifies concerns and causes of problems and finds links between information from various sources.

Can you think of a recent situation you faced which required analytic thinking on your part?

What has been one of the most challenging situations which required your analysis?

Have you ever identified a potential problem or opportunity that your manager or others had not seen? Tell me about a time this happened.

Have you ever been in a situation where there has been a recurring problem at work? Tell me about it. What did you do in this situation?

(Also consider analytic reasoning/cognitive ability tests to assess this competency.)

Achievement orientation: Demonstrates motivation to achieve results; perseveres with plans.

What has been a particularly demanding goal for you to achieve?

What have been the accomplishments in your present position of which you are most proud? Choose one the candidate mentions: *This sounds interesting – tell me about it.*

What would be an example of a goal or a task you have had which has presented the most obstacles for you?

(If the candidate is a recent graduate) *Which aspects of completing your degree were the most difficult to overcome?*

(This competency might also be assessed through reviewing accomplishments on the résumé/application form.)

Conscientiousness: Works steadily, efficiently and dependably; checks work thoroughly for errors/omissions.

What tasks have been a regular part of your duties? How have you gone about accomplishing task X? What happens when it is complete?

We all have times of not being able to complete everything we want to by the end of a day. Could you think of a recent example?

In which aspects of your work is it most important to make no errors? What have you done to try to prevent errors?

Which aspects of your work must be done on time? What have you done to meet time deadlines?

(This competency can also be assessed well through the reference check.)

Creativity: Develops innovative solutions to work-related problems; identifies potential opportunities and ways to capitalize on them.

Can you think of a situation in which an innovative course of action was needed? What did you do in this situation?

Have you seen any opportunities to improve productivity/sales/the way work gets done in your present (or recent) job? What did you do about it?

Customer service orientation: Is courteous, patient, pleasant, and helpful with customers; shows understanding for customers' concerns; takes actions to accommodate customer needs whenever possible.

I am interested in your day-to-day experience with customers in your present job. Can you pick a recent customer interaction you've had and tell me about it?

What are the typical customer interactions you have in your present position? Can you think of a recent example of one of these?

Can you think of a time you received particularly positive feedback about a customer interaction you have had? Tell me about it.

How about a situation in which a customer was unhappy with the way he or she was treated by you?

Can you think of a time when you have had to deal with the concerns of a particularly challenging customer?

Decision making: Identifies a variety of alternatives before selecting a course of action, weighs advantages and disadvantages of each alternative, and chooses a logical course of action based on available information and reasonable assumptions.

What has been a recent decision you have had to make in your present position? Tell me about the decision you faced.

Can you think of a particularly challenging decision you have had to make? We have all made some decisions or recommendations we wish we could do over again. Can you give me an example where this has happened to you?

Can you think of a situation where you have had to decide how to resolve a problem in your work area? What did you do in this situation?

(This competency can also be assessed well through the reference check.)

Delegating: Considers job responsibilities, workloads, skills, and developmental needs in effectively allocating work among staff. Communicates specific work expectations while delegating tasks, discusses ways of accomplishing tasks, and follows up to ensure successful task completion.

Think of a staff member whom you currently supervise and to whom you have delegated responsibility for important areas of work. What sorts of responsibility did you give to this person? How did you delegate these responsibilities? How did this work out?

Which staff member in your section/unit have you trusted most to follow through on delegated responsibilities? Can you give me an example of something you delegated to him/her?

How about someone who did not perform effectively on a responsibility you delegated to him/her? What was the situation?

Flexibility: Maintains high level of performance under changing conditions, tasks, responsibilities, or people.

What is one of the largest changes that has affected the way you work in your present position?

What kinds of situations have occurred on your job which required you to be flexible?

Have you ever been in a situation where you have had to take on new tasks or roles? Describe this situation and what you did.

(Focus on a major transition indicated in the candidate's résumé, such as from one organization to another, moving departments within the same organization, from undergraduate school to graduate school, from working in the home to working in an organization.) *In going from ____ to ___, what did you find to be the most different? What did you do to make the transition?*

High work standards: Establishes high goals for self and others. Seeks challenging assignments and demonstrates willingness to learn new tasks and perform a variety of duties.

In your present position, what standards have you set for doing a good job? How did you determine them?

What performance discussions have you had with your manager?
(OR)
Tell me about your most recent performance discussion with your manager. What aspects of your performance did you talk about? How did you and your manager view your performance on these aspects?

What contributions to your department/organization are you most proud of?

Most work has to be done to certain levels of performance, such as within time-frames, to particular levels of quality and quantity. What have been the most challenging standards in your present position? To what responsibilities do those standards apply? Who set those standards? What have you done to try to achieve those standards?

(This competency can also be assessed well through the reference check.)

Initiative: Takes actions to achieve favourable outcomes for the organization, beyond minimum performance expectations, and seeks opportunities to improve work procedures.

What assignments/projects/tasks did you take on since you've had the position? How did you come to take on these tasks?

How has your job changed since you started? Who initiated each of these changes? How was each one initiated?

Have you done things in your job beyond what has been required? Tell me about some things which you've done that exceeded requirements.

Can you think of a policy or procedure in your department/organization which you thought needed changing? What did you do about it?

(For a managerial position) *When taking on your present position, were there any areas of your section's performance that you believed needed improvement? What did you do?*

(There may be evidence of initiative, or missed opportunities for initiative, in behavioural descriptions provided by the candidate for other competencies. This competency can also be assessed well through the reference check.)

Keeping informed: Maintains an awareness of events and changes inside and outside of the organization, and advances in one's professional field.

What changes inside your present organization do you believe are having the greatest impact on your area of responsibility? How have you kept informed of them?

What events outside your present organization do you believe are having the greatest impact on your field? What is the latest information you remember reading or hearing about that event?

How have you kept up to date on what your company's competitors are doing?

What do you read in your field? Can you think of the most recent article in _____ (journal, magazine, paper) you've read? Seminars attended in the past ____ years?

(Note: This competency involves an ongoing activity more than responding to particular situations, and so these questions do not fit the situation-behaviour-outcome framework.)

People management: Enlists support, cooperation and participation when influencing and guiding others toward the accomplishment of tasks. Monitors performance on an ongoing basis, provides positive feedback for effective performance, coaches to resolve performance difficulties.

How do you manage the performance of those who report to you? (You might focus on a staff member [or group] who has been easy to manage and one who has been difficult to manage, asking about memorable situations.)

Can you tell me about a situation in which you attempted to raise an individual's (or group's) level of performance?

Can you please describe a situation in which you had to get your staff to implement a policy or decision that they did not agree with?

What changes have you introduced in your section (i.e., department, division) since you became its manager? (Focus on one change) *What was the situation that led you to make that change? How did you introduce it?*

What are the most critical performance criteria for your section? How have you monitored the performance of your section in these areas?

Planning: Plans actions to accomplish goals systematically, including establishing time-frames, allocating resources, and following up on details.

What has been one of the most challenging goals you have worked on accomplishing recently? How did you go about it? (Look for evidence/lack of planning.)

Can you describe a project you have implemented? (Look for or ask about planning.)

Can you think of times in your job in which many things need to be done at once (or work needed to be accomplished under tight time or resource constraints)? (This question can also be used to assess the candidate's time management.)

Relations with others: Is pleasant, cooperative, and gets along well with others. Keeps manager informed, reports problems promptly, and seeks guidance when needed. Develops and maintains a network of personal contacts within the organization.

What people in your present position do you work with most frequently? Which ones do you get along with best? Can you think of an example of an interaction with _____ which typifies how you get along with him/her? Which people do you find more difficult to get along with? How about an example of an interaction with _____ which typifies the difficulty?

When was the last time you had to ask someone from another department for something?

We all find some people difficult to work with. Can you think of one of the more difficult people you have had to work with?

Self-confidence: Asserts own point of view, even when it differs from others (e.g., manager's); shows confidence in own skills and capacity to complete tasks; seeks necessary resources for self and/or staff to work effectively.

We've all been in the situation where what we believe is best is different from what our manager or peers want, or what has been standard operating procedure in the past. Can you think of a situation like this that you have faced?

Have you ever had to make a strong case to someone for resources you needed?

Tell me about a time where you have had to make a verbal presentation to a group of your peers or superiors? How did you handle this situation? (Look for evidence of confidence in tackling the situation.)

(This competency may also be assessed based on the candidate's behaviour in the interview.)

Sensitivity: Demonstrates an awareness of others' concerns, interests and positions, and takes into consideration the impact that decisions and plans are likely to have on them.

What aspects of what you do in your present position affect other people you work with in your section (or in another department)? Can you think of a recent situation in which what you did affected others?

Which people are most affected by the decisions or actions you take? (focusing on one person/group.) *What affects them? How are they affected? Can you give me a recent example where your doing this affected them?*

We all have had to work with people who see things differently from us. Can you think of a person or group you have worked with who saw things quite differently from you? How about an example of when they didn't agree with what you were doing?

(For managerial position.) *Can you give me an example of a recent discussion you've had with a staff member over a performance problem?*

(For responses to all of the questions for this competency, look for evidence/lack of sensitivity.)

Stability: Performs stably while under pressure or in a changing work environment.

Virtually all jobs have stresses associated with them. What kinds of pressures or stresses have you faced in your present position?

When was the last time you remember getting frustrated or impatient with someone at work?

What have been the most sudden or major changes in your present job?

How has your job changed since you took it on? Which of these changes have you found to be the most unsettling?

(This competency can also be assessed well through the reference check.)

Technical skill/knowledge: Demonstrates sufficient level of understanding and skill in required technical area.

The specific content of this dimension needs to be defined for each job, and interview questions for this competency are usually asked by someone with the necessary technical expertise (e.g., the manager to whom the position reports, rather than a personnel specialist).

Questions for this competency can focus on behavioural descriptions of past experience and training as well as checking candidates' understanding of technical aspects of the job. Here is an example of two behavioural description questions designed for a computer programmer position, but which could easily be adapted for other positions involving technical skill/knowledge:

Here at XYZ company, we usually write computer programs using the _____ language. Have you developed programs using this language? What is the most recent (or most involved) program you've written in the _____ language? What features of the language did you use for that program?

I see on your résumé that you attended training in the _____ aspect of programming. Can you give me more details of what that course involved? What/how did you do in that course?

Questions to check a candidate's knowledge in technical areas usually involve having the candidate explain processes, characteristics, etc., such as the following question for a milk process control operator:

And how is milk pressure maintained at a constant level at this stage of processing?

In addition to asking for technical understanding in the interview, the candidate can be given a tour of the technical work area, in which the interviewer assesses technical knowledge through the discussion.

Verbal communication: Expresses ideas orally with clarity, appropriate grammar, pace and non-verbal gestures; listens effectively.

What aspects of your present job have involved the most verbal communication with other people?
(OR)
In what areas of your present job has good verbal communication been most important?

(Only if group presentations are required) *Have you ever made presentations to groups? What has been your most challenging group presentation?* or *What was the largest group presentation you have made?*

(This competency may also be assessed based on the candidate's behaviour in the interview.)

Written communication: Expresses ideas in writing clearly, with correct grammar and spelling, and in a well-organized way.

What has been the nature of the writing you have done in your present position? Can you tell me about a recent example of _____?

What have been the most complex reports (letters, minutes, proposals, business plans, etc.) you have written? Can you give me an example of ____?

What have you written recently?

(Also consider asking to see examples of the candidate's written work.)

G

EXAMPLES OF BDI INTERVIEW SCHEDULES

In this section we present three illustrations of behavioural description interview questions, for three different positions. The first illustration is for the position of Project Leader. Because this job was new to the organization, competencies were inferred from tasks, rather than from a critical incident job analysis. A full outline of the competencies required for the position is presented, followed by the BDI interview schedule.

For the second illustration, for a Hospital Charge Nurse position, competencies were derived from a critical incident analysis. The third example, a Government Planner/Analyst position, was based on a combination of critical incidents and competencies inferred from job tasks because the position was in the process of evolving in the organization.

In order to avoid redundancy, notes for opening and closing the interview are only included in the first of these three interview schedules.

POSITION 1: PROJECT LEADER, PERFORMANCE MANAGEMENT SYSTEM (PMS)

COMPETENCIES

People management: Enlists support, cooperation and participation when influencing and guiding others toward the accomplishment of tasks. Monitors performance on an ongoing basis, providing positive feedback for effective performance, and coaches to resolve performance difficulties.

The Project Leader must interact with many individuals, including various levels of management over whom s/he has no direct control (i.e. no reporting relationship). The Project Leader must secure resources essential for the project, such as personnel time and access to necessary records. Effective influence skills include clearly explaining the purpose of projects, acknowledging others' priorities and time-frames, seeking others' ideas for solving problems and generating ideas, and acknowledging others' support in both informal and written reports.

The success of this project will result, in part, from the commitment obtained to it through the Project Leader's involvement of others throughout the organization. Leadership must be demonstrated on both an individual and small group basis.

Planning: Plans actions to accomplish goals systematically, including establishing time-frames, allocating resources, and following up on details.

The development, implementation, and evaluation of the PMS will involve many interdependent tasks and people. The Project Leader must plan carefully how and when tasks are assigned, budget resources appropriately, and establish control procedures to ensure that tasks are completed on time and to quality standards.

PMS knowledge/experience: Demonstrates sufficient level of understanding and skill in *performance management/appraisal and general human resource management.*

High work standards: Establishes high goals for self and others. Seeks challenging assignments and demonstrates willingness to learn new tasks and perform a variety of duties.

The PMS project must be completed within tight time deadlines. Most of the quality standards for the project must be established by the Project Leader, and our organization is expecting a well-researched and executed project. The Project Leader must carry out the PMS development project with little direct supervision, and consequently s/he must take the initiative to establish high standards for her/himself, the project and project team.

Analytic thinking: Identifies concerns and causes of problems and finds links between information from various sources.

A great deal of information, both within our organization (e.g. past performance problems that the PMS is expected to solve) and external to the organization (e.g. PMSs that have been implemented elsewhere) must be reviewed to develop the most appropriate PMS for the organization. The Project Leader must determine what information to investigate and prioritize information that will be given to the team to review.

Decision making: Identifies a variety of alternatives before selecting a course of action, weighs advantages and disadvantages of each alternative, and chooses a logical course of action based on available information and reasonable assumptions.

The Project Leader must make a number of decisions that will be crucial to the successful implementation of the PMS, including who will be recommended as other project team members, specific aspects of the proposed PMS, and how the PMS will be implemented and evaluated.

Verbal communication: Expresses ideas orally with clarity, appropriate grammar, pace and non-verbal gestures; and listens effectively.

This position involves frequent verbal communication individually, in small groups, and in large, formal presentations. Much of the Project Leader's verbal communication individually and in small groups will be on an informal, ad hoc *basis, involving minimal preparation. The perceived credibility of the PMS and project team will be based partially on the professionalism and quality of the Project Leader's verbal communication.*

Written communication: Expresses ideas in writing clearly and grammatically, and in a well-organized way.

The Project Leader must submit to general management progress reports and proposals that are clear and succinct. S/he must also provide written communications to our employees, e.g. brief articles in the organization's newsletter. The quality of the Project Leader's writing is expected to have substantial influence on the acceptance of the proposed PMS.

BDI SCHEDULE FOR PROJECT LEADER, PMS

Applicant's Name: _____

Interviewer's Name: _____

Position Sought: *Project Leader, PMS*

Date: _____

(Note: The following are only examples *of questions you could ask to elicit information about various job competencies.)*

Introduction and background information

Greet applicant, explain purpose of the interview, describe the plan for the interview and that you will be taking notes.

Make sure you have general background information by following up on application form/résumé.

What are your specific reasons for seeking this job? In other words, how do you hope to benefit from this job?

Competencies

People management: Enlists support, cooperation and participation when influencing and guiding others toward the accomplishment of tasks. Monitors performance on an ongoing basis, providing positive feedback for effective performance and coaches to resolve performance difficulties.

Have you ever managed a project team? Describe the project you managed, the people, and what you accomplished.

Situation –

Behaviour –

Outcome –

Can you think of any other projects?

Situation –

Behaviour –

Outcome –

Have you ever been in a position of trying to influence an entire organization or a large group to adopt a recommendation or plan?

Situation –

Behaviour –

Outcome –

Describe a situation where you have convinced a group of people or a manager that your method for accomplishing a task was best. Describe how you got them to go along with you.

Situation –

Behaviour –

Outcome –

What experience do you have in leading group meetings? Did any involve leading a group of professionals and managers with differing views? Describe a recent situation.

Situation –

Behaviour –

Outcome –

Planning: Plans actions to accomplish goals, including establishing time-frames and allocating resources.

Have you ever planned a major project? What was it?

Situation –

Behaviour –

Outcome –

Can you think of a project you have implemented?

Situation –

Behaviour –

Outcome –

PMS knowledge/experience: Demonstrates sufficient level of understanding and skill in performance management/appraisal and general human resource management.

What has been your exposure to performance management/appraisal systems?

What has been your experience in the area of human resource management?

High work standards: Establishes high goals for self and others. Seeks challenging assignments and demonstrates willingness to learn new tasks and perform a variety of duties.

In your present position, what standards have you set for doing a good job? How did you determine them?
What have been the most challenging standards in your present position?

   Situation –

   Behaviour –

   Outcome –

What contributions to your department are you most proud of?

   Situation –

   Behaviour –

   Outcome –

Analytic thinking: Identifies concerns and causes of problems and finds links between information from various sources.

What has been one of the most challenging situations which required your analysis?

   Situation –

   Behaviour –

   Outcome –

Developing a performance management system will involve reading about and analysing many potential systems. What other projects have you worked on that have involved analysing and synthesizing a great deal of information?

Situation –

Behaviour –

Outcome –

Have you ever researched an issue by consulting library sources as well as members of other organizations? What was the situation?

Situation –

Behaviour –

Outcome –

Decision making: Identifies a variety of alternatives before selecting a course of action, weighs advantages and disadvantages of each alternative, and chooses a logical course of action based on available information and logical assumptions.

What has been a recent decision you have had to make in your present position?

Situation –

Behaviour –

Outcome –

We all have made some decisions or recommendations we wish we could do over again. Can you think of one you wish you decided differently?

Situation –

Behaviour –

Outcome –

Verbal communication: Expresses ideas orally with clarity, appropriate grammar, pace and non-verbal gestures; and listens effectively.

What has been one of the biggest challenges you have faced when making presentations to groups?

Situation –

Behaviour –

Outcome –

Any other instances that you can think of?

Situation –

Behaviour –

Outcome –

What would be one of the most complex processes or systems you have had to explain to other people?

Situation –

Behaviour –

Outcome –

Written communication: Expresses ideas in writing clearly and with appropriate grammar.

What types of writing have you done in your career? Can you give me an example of each?

Situation –

Behaviour –

Outcome –

What kinds of reports have you written? How many? Can you give me an example of one of the more complex reports you have written?

Situation –

Behaviour –

Outcome –

What is the most recent proposal you have written?

Situation –

Behaviour –

Outcome –

Question to take time to look over notes

I appreciate your giving me so much information. I'd like you to take a minute or so to think of questions you have about the position, while I double check my notes.

(During this time, review your notes. Check to see that all behavioural descriptions are complete and look for any other questions you could ask.)

Candidate's questions

Closing

POSITION 2: HOSPITAL CHARGE NURSE

BDI SCHEDULE FOR HOSPITAL CHARGE NURSE POSITION

(Note: The following competencies have been derived from the critical incident job analysis of this position outlined in section C. Again, the questions listed here are simply examples of ones you could ask to elicit information about various job competencies.)

People management: Enlists support, cooperation and participation when influencing and guiding others toward the accomplishment of tasks. Negotiates with patients, staff, peers, doctors and senior management in order to achieve the optimal outcome for all concerned. Monitors performance on an ongoing basis, providing positive feedback for effective performance and coaches to resolve performance difficulties. Acts as an advocate for staff.

More often than not, nurses are required to complete a lot of paper work on their job, which they do not really like doing. Tell me about the most challenging but necessary set of documentations that you have had to introduce to your staff.

Situation –

Behaviour –

Outcome –

Doctors from both within and outside the hospital can transfer patients into your ward. Sometimes the ward may already be full. Has this happened to you? Tell me about the hardest negotiation that you have had to make with a doctor who insisted on having his/her patients transferred into your ward.

Situation –

Behaviour –

Outcome –

We all know that there are times when staff do not perform up to standard. Can you recall a time when a member of your staff did something which was below the required standard of performance. Please tell me what happened.

Situation –

Behaviour –

Outcome –

Initiative: Realizes the need for change and seeks feasible solutions. Takes actions to achieve favourable outcomes for the organization, beyond minimum performance expectations, and seeks opportunities to improve work procedures.

It is very important to discover opportunities for the hospital to improve its current operations and provision of quality patient care. Tell me about an opportunity you initiated in your most recent job.

Situation –

Behaviour –

Outcome –

Sometimes there are processes or systems in place which cause problems because they are not working at their best, or they require further updating and modifying to suit users' needs. Tell me about the biggest problem caused by a process or system that you faced in your last job.

Situation –

Behaviour –

Outcome –

Patient care: Ensures patient safety and provision of high quality patient care, shows concern for the patient and their family, and provides help and support for them and any decisions that they make.

We are all aware that different patients require different medical and emotional care. Can you tell me about a time when a patient wanted your support in a decision that s/he has made which was not in accordance with strict medical practice?

Situation –

Behaviour –

Outcome –

Friends and family of patients often go through a great deal of stress and emotional difficulties because of the pain and suffering their loved ones experience. One common way for them to let off steam is by expressing anger and discontent towards staff. Tell me about the most difficult family member that you have had to deal with.

Situation –

Behaviour –

Outcome –

Open communication: Develops and maintains open communication channels with all staff. Distributes and interprets (when necessary) information from, and decisions by, senior management.

Management often pass information to Charge Nurses through memoranda, newsletters and management meetings. It is important that staff in the ward receive this information. However, busy staff may not take the time to read and digest a lot of written information. Describe a situation in your last job where you were responsible for ensuring that information was disseminated and understood.

Situation –

Behaviour –

Outcome –

Often in a hospital setting, conflicts occur between individuals (e.g., between two staff members), or between groups (e.g., staff and management). Describe the most challenging conflict situation that you have faced. What did you do?

Situation –

Behaviour –

Outcome –

Staff selection and development: Assesses technical and interpersonal fit of applicants in selection interviews, facilitates the integration of new staff, and shows commitment to employee development.
New employees often need some support in building work relationships and integrating into new work environments. Tell me about the last employee you hired. How did you assist this person to settle into his/her new position?

Situation –

Behaviour –

Outcome –

During a selection interview, it is very easy to choose the wrong person because of various types of interviewer bias, either personal or technical. Have you ever made a dissatisfying decision because you strongly believed in your personal opinions, or gut feelings about the applicant?

Situation –

Behaviour –

Outcome –

Planning and organization: Establishes courses of action to accomplish goals, including establishing time-frames and allocating resources. Demonstrates fairness in designing rosters, makes assessments of work-loads and allocates staff accordingly.

Can you think of a time in your job when work needed to be accomplished under tight time or resource constraints? Describe the situation and how you dealt with it.

Situation –

Behaviour –

Outcome –

It is important that staff feel happy about the shifts that they have been assigned to do. There are times when they want preferential rosters to be specifically made for them because of circumstances which they feel are justifiable. Tell me about the most difficult decision that you have had to make about whether or not a preferential roster should be granted.

Situation –

Behaviour –

Outcome –

POSITION 3: GOVERNMENT PLANNER/ANALYST

Reporting relationships

The planner/analyst will report to the Section Manager, Environmental Planning.

Principal function

To develop and undertake with minimal supervision, particular investigations, plan preparation or work functions of a coordinating, presenting and policy development nature.

Key tasks/responsibilities (in order of importance)

Analysing and developing policies, plans, proposals, strategies and statements.
Liaising and consulting with public, special interest groups, and peers.
Writing technical reports, policies, plans, proposals, strategies and statements.
Managing Project Teams assembled for specific tasks.
Conducting social and environmental research.

Competencies (Derived from a critical incident job analysis)

Analytic thinking: Identifies concerns and causes of problems and finds links between information from various sources.

The planner/analyst is required to develop and review proposals, plans, and policies. S/he must be able to sort through large amounts of information, break down complex situations into their key elements, determine what is relevant and irrelevant, identify various solutions or options, analyse the pros and cons of the options, and weigh the options against one another.

Planning: Establishes courses of action to accomplish goals, including establishing time-frames and allocating resources.

The planner/analyst is required to work on complex projects that may last several months in duration. S/he may also be required to work on several projects over the same time period. Many of these projects have time-frames that are determined by external circumstances and must be met. The ability to plan a project, set milestones, meet deadlines, and allocate resources within budgetary restraints is essential.

Technical knowledge: Demonstrates sufficient level of understanding and skill required in project management techniques, resource management, planning techniques, and relevant legislation.

The planner/analyst will be required to work in or lead project teams, and to apply planning techniques to develop resource management programmes consistent with legislative requirements.

Written communication: Expresses ideas in writing clearly and with appropriate grammar.

The planner/analyst must produce written reports, often of considerable length and detail, on somewhat technical topics. S/he must be able to write clearly and concisely in the language of the profession. S/he must also be able to present complex or technical ideas in layperson's language. The ability to write for particular audiences is desirable.

People management: Enlists support, cooperation and participation when influencing and guiding others toward the accomplishment of tasks. Monitors performance on an ongoing basis, providing positive feedback for effective performance and coaches to resolve performance difficulties.

The planner/analyst must interact with many people and groups both internal and external to the organization. Often s/he will be required to coordinate the work or contributions of others to a specific project. The ability to fruitfully liaise with and or manage other persons or groups is necessary to the position.

Verbal communication: Expresses ideas orally with clarity, appropriate grammar, pace and non-verbal gestures; listens effectively.

This position involves frequent verbal communication individually, in small groups, and in large, formal presentations. Much of the planner/analyst's verbal communication individually and in small groups will be on an informal, ad hoc basis, involving minimal preparation. In larger formal presentations the planner/analyst will be responsible for representing the organization to Council, Council Committees, Planning Tribunals and public or special interest group meetings. Much of the organization's and the planner/analyst's credibility will be determined by the quality and professionalism of his/her verbal communication.

Teamwork: Works cooperatively and effectively in a team situation.

The planner/analyst is frequently required to work in formal or ad hoc teams or groups on particular projects. The ability to cooperate and willingness to communicate freely and regularly are important aspects of the position.

Decision making: Identifies a variety of alternatives before selecting a course of action, weighs advantages and disadvantages of each alternative and chooses a course of action based on logical assumptions.

The planner/analyst will be required to make decisions as a regular part of his/her work. S/he must be able justify decisions and recommendations to Councils, Committees and public groups etc. through sound logical reasoning.

Initiative: Takes actions to achieve favourable outcomes for the organization, beyond minimum performance expectations, and seeks opportunities to improve work procedures.

In a changing cultural, legal, and technological environment opportunities for developing new and innovative methods and procedures are constantly arising. The initiative to perceive opportunities as they arise and to autonomously act upon them is a valuable attribute for planner/analysts.

Creativity: Develops innovative solutions to work-related problems and identifies potential business opportunities and ways to capitalise on them.

In the course of their work, planner/analysts are confronted by many complex social, cultural, environmental and bureaucratic problems. The ability to see beyond the immediate confines of the problems, and a subsequent narrow range of solutions, to new creative and innovative approaches and solutions is a valuable skill for this position.

Sensitivity: Demonstrates an awareness of others' concerns, interests and positions. Is sensitive to political and cultural issues.

The end result of the planner/analyst's work may affect many people and groups in the community. It is, therefore, necessary that s/he be sensitive to the needs and concerns of these people and groups. Planner/analysts must be aware of, and sensitive to, political and cultural issues. They must be familiar with, and practise, appropriate protocols and processes of consultation.

BDI SCHEDULE FOR GOVERNMENT PLANNER/ANALYST

Competencies

Analytic thinking: Identifies concerns and causes of problems and finds links between information from various sources.

One aspect of a planner/analyst's work involves the analysis of proposals, plans or situations. Have you had any recent experience involving similar analytical work? What was the task? What did you do?

Situation –

Behaviour –

Outcome –

Collecting, categorizing and analysing data and information for research purposes is another component of the planner/analyst position. Have you collected and analysed data previously? Have you conducted research? What tasks have you done that have required these skills?

Situation –

Behaviour –

Outcome –

Have you ever identified a potential problem or opportunity that your manager or others had not seen? Tell me about a time this happened.

Situation –

Behaviour –

Outcome –

(You might also consider using a test to measure analytical reasoning.)

Planning: Plans actions to accomplish goals, including establishing timeframes and allocating resources.

As a planner/analyst, the need to prepare ad hoc *reports with little prior notice may arise in an already pressured time schedule. Have you ever found yourself in a similar situation, faced with completing an unexpected urgent task with little or no time remaining free? What was the situation? What did you do?*

Situation –

Behaviour –

Outcome –

Planner/analysts may have to plan, organize and implement major projects lasting several months. Have you ever planned a major project? What was it? How did you go about it?

Situation –

Behaviour –

Outcome –

Describe your activities on a recent day that you remember as being especially busy.

Situation –

Behaviour –

Outcome –

Technical knowledge: Demonstrates sufficient level of understanding and skill required in: project management techniques, resource management, planning techniques, and relevant legislation.

Describe a project or situation in which you were involved that required knowledge of resource management law. What particular part of the legislation was involved? What did you do?

Situation –

Behaviour –

Outcome –

What computer applications have you used in the course of your work? Tell me about what you did with (name one of the applications mentioned). *Did you experience any difficulties using this application? What did you do about it?*

Situation –

Behaviour –

Outcome –

(Technical qualifications, previous work experience, and referees may help assess this competency.)

People management: Enlists support, cooperation and participation when influencing and guiding others toward the accomplishment of tasks. Monitors performance on an ongoing basis, providing positive feedback for effective performance and coaches to resolve performance difficulties.

Planner/analysts are sometimes required to manage project teams. Have you ever managed a project team? Describe the project you managed, the people, and what you accomplished.

Situation –

Behaviour –

Outcome –

Can you describe any other situation where you have had to obtain the support and cooperation of other people in order to complete a task or project? What did you do in this situation?

Situation –

Behaviour –

Outcome –

We do not always agree with the decisions of our peers or managers. Tell me of a time that you have disagreed with a peer or manager. What did you disagree with? Did you do anything about it?

Situation –

Behaviour –

Outcome –

Have you ever been in a position of trying to influence a large group or even an entire organization to adopt a recommendation or plan? How did you proceed?

Situation –

Behaviour –

Outcome –

What experience have you had in leading group meetings? Did any involve leading a group of professionals and managers with differing views? Describe a recent situation.

Situation –

Behaviour –

Outcome –

(Also consider using referees to help assess this competency.)

Verbal communication: Expresses ideas orally with clarity, appropriate grammar, pace and non-verbal gestures; and listens effectively.

Have you ever made presentations to groups? What has been one of the biggest challenges you have faced in making presentations to groups?

Situation –

Behaviour –

Outcome –

What are some of the most complex processes or information you have had to explain to other people?

Situation –

Behaviour –

Outcome –

(This competency may be assessed throughout the interview.)

Written communication: Expresses ideas in writing clearly and with appropriate grammar.

What kinds of reports have you written? Can you give me some examples? What is the most recent proposal you have written? What has been one of the most challenging reports you have written? How was it challenging?

(Consider asking the applicant to bring an example of his/her work to the interview.)

Teamwork: Works cooperatively and effectively in a team situation.

Planner/analysts are frequently required to work on projects in teams. Describe a team project that you have worked on. What was your role in the team? What did you do to gain cooperation among team members?

Situation –

Behaviour –

Outcome –

Have you ever had any conflicts with other members of a team in which you were working? What was the conflicting issue? What did you do about the conflict?

Situation –

Behaviour –

Outcome –

Decision making: Identifies a variety of alternatives before selecting a course of action, weighs advantages and disadvantages of each alternative and chooses a course of action based on logical assumptions.

What is one of the biggest decisions you have made this past year? How did you go about making the decision? What alternatives did you consider?

Situation –

Behaviour –

Outcome –

What day-to-day decisions do you face on your present job? Can you give me an example of one that you have faced in the past week?

Situation –

Behaviour –

Outcome –

Sometimes, when faced with a decision about an issue, we may have to choose between a safe alternative with minimal returns, and a more risky alternative with greater potential returns. Have you ever been in this situation? Describe the details for me.

Situation –

Behaviour –

Outcome –

Initiative: Takes actions to achieve favourable outcomes for the organization, beyond minimum performance expectations, and seeks opportunities to improve work procedures.

What projects have you initiated in your previous/current employment? Why did you consider the project necessary? How did you go about initiating the project? What was the outcome?

Situation –

Behaviour –

Outcome –

Can you think of a business opportunity that you perceived during the course of your work. What did you do about it?

Situation –

Behaviour –

Outcome –

Can you think of a policy or procedure in your previous/current organization which you thought needed changing? What did you do about it?

Situation –

Behaviour –

Outcome –

Creativity: Develops innovative solutions to work-related problems and identifies potential business opportunities and ways to capitalize on them.

Have you ever developed an innovative or creative solution to a problem that you encountered at work? Describe the problem. What was your solution?

Situation –

Behaviour –

Outcome –

What do you consider to be your most creative piece of work? How did it come about?

Situation –

Behaviour –

Outcome –

Sensitivity: Demonstrates an awareness of others' concerns, interests and positions; sensitive to political and cultural issues.

Have you ever consulted with community groups regarding the development of a plan or proposal? How did you go about the process of consultation? Did any difficulties arise? What did you do about them?

Situation –

Behaviour –

Outcome –

Which people are affected most by the decisions or actions you take? (Focusing on one person/group) *What affects them? How are they affected? Can you give a recent example where your decisions affected them?*

Situation –

Behaviour –

Outcome –

H
SAMPLE FORM FOR INTEGRATING INTERVIEWERS' RATINGS

Position_____ Candidate: _____

Competency	Panel Member 1	Panel Member 2	Panel Member 3	Consensus/ Av. Rating
Competency 1				
Competency 2				
Competency 3				
Competency 4				
Competency 5				
Competency 6				

Note: A form such as this one could be used to record individual panel members' (i.e., interviewers') ratings and the final (consensus or average) ratings for each candidate.

Example for the position of Project Leader, Performance Management Systems:

Position: *Project Leader, PMS*   Candidate: *Chris Sanders*

Competency	Interviewers			Consensus Rating
	F. Smith	*D. McGrath*	*S. Hastings*	
People mgmt.	3	3	4	3
Planning	3	2	3	3
PMS knowledge	5	4	4	4
High standards	4	3	4	3
Analyt. thkng.	4	3	4	3
Dec. making	3	3	3	3
Verbal comm.	4	4	3	4
Written comm.	3	3	3	3

I

SAMPLE FORM FOR COMPARING CANDIDATE RATINGS

Position: _____

Competency	Weight	(Candidate 1) Rtng (Wtd Rtng)	(Candidate 2) Rtng (Wtd Rtng)	(Candidate 3) Rtng (Wtd Rtng)
Competency 1	( )	( )	( )	( )
Competency 2	( )	( )	( )	( )
Competency 3	( )	( )	( )	( )
Competency 4	( )	( )	( )	( )
Competency 5	( )	( )	( )	( )
Competency 6	( )	( )	( )	( )

Total Weighted Ratings: ____   ____   ____

Note: With weighted competencies, candidates can be compared by multiplying competency weights by interview ratings and summing weighted ratings for each candidate.

Example for the position of Project Leader, Performance Management Systems:

Position: *Project Leader, PMS*

Competency	Weight	C. Sanders Rtng (Wtd Rtng)		K. Appleton Rtng (Wtd Rtng)		G. Thompson Rtng (Wtd Rtng)	
People mgmt.	(5)	3	(15)	4	(20)	3	(15)
Planning	(4)	3	(12)	5	(20)	3	(12)
PMS knowledge	(4)	4	(16)	3	(12)	2	(8)
High standards	(3)	3	(9)	4	(12)	3	(9)
Analyt. thkng.	(3)	3	(9)	4	(12)	3	(9)
Dec. making	(3)	3	(9)	3	(9)	3	(9)
Verbal comm.	(3)	4	(12)	4	(12)	3	(9)
Written comm.	(3)	3	(9)	4	(12)	4	(12)
Total Weighted Ratings		91		109		83	

Weights and weighted ratings are shown here for illustration purposes only. In this particular example, no competencies have been weighted as at least twice as important as others, and therefore weights are not really necessary. A final decision could be made by simply comparing rating profiles across candidates, or by adding or averaging ratings for each candidate.

J

EXAMPLE OF A SITUATIONAL INTERVIEW SCHEDULE

Position: Hospital Charge Nurse

Two questions for each of six competencies were developed for this position. A scoring key is provided under each question, where 1 represents a weak answer, 3 an acceptable answer, and 5 a superior answer.

Competencies

People management: Enlists support, cooperation and participation when influencing and guiding others toward the accomplishment of tasks. Negotiates with patients, staff, peers, doctors and senior management in order to achieve the optimal outcome for all concerned. Monitors performance on an ongoing basis, providing positive feedback for effective performance and coaches to resolve performance difficulties. Acts as an advocate for staff.

1. *It is just before Christmas. Two staff members contact you advising of their absence from tomorrow night's shift. Both have legitimate reasons for being unable to come. Your ward will be unstaffed. How would you approach resolving this problem?*

    1 – We have a pool of nurses in this hospital. They should find staff to cover.

    or

    Accept unavailability. Leave agency to cover.

    or

    Inform them that they both must come to work.

3 – Contact my manager and discuss the situation. Look at the possibility of moving patients to another ward or contacting agency.

or

Try and get the two staff members to negotiate with each other, so that only one person is absent, and replace the other with an agency nurse.

5 – Notify my manager and discuss the situation. Check availability of alternative staff on ward and beyond, negotiate replacements to ensure the night is covered, even if this leaves a shortage on the day shift. Contact agency and discuss available options for cover. If no success with agency or a ward in my own division, then contact part-timers or casual workers to see if they could cover. If not, check duty roster and try to negotiate replacements. Look at the possibility of moving patients to another ward. If all else fails, do the shift myself.

2. *A night nurse on a ward has been upsetting patients with verbal abuse. The Charge Nurse confronted the night nurse about the situation. He said that he had been having difficulty at home and was under considerable stress and had not realized that he had been upsetting the patients. After this discussion the night nurse's behaviour improved for a few weeks. However, the Charge Nurse has begun receiving complaints about him again. It seems that he is slipping back to his previous bad habits. As Charge Nurse, what action would you take in these circumstances?*

1 – Tell the nurse off in no uncertain terms. Suggest that he shape up or look for another ward to work in.

or

Talk to nurse again but do not take any further action.

or

Base nurse's performance appraisal on this behaviour.

3 – Talk to nurse again. Take him off night shift. Explain reasons for doing so.

or

Go through discussion process with nurse again. Give him a second chance, but with a verbal warning, outline consequences of continuing unacceptable behaviour.

5 – Investigate fully. Discuss the complaints with the staff member involved as soon as possible. Inform that behaviour is

unacceptable. Ask for his explanation. Remind them that this is not the first time that complaints have been made. Advise the nurse that he may/will need to be taken off night duty and a performance review initiated. Perhaps he needs some help with the issues affecting his performance. Ask nurse about stress situation. Suggest possible sources of help (e.g., Employee Assistance Programme). If accepted, refer on and monitor situation for an agreed period. If rejected, may need to issue a written warning and take the initial steps of the official disciplinary process.

Initiative: Realizes the need for change and seeks feasible solutions. Takes actions to achieve favourable outcomes for the organization, beyond minimum performance expectations, and seeks opportunities to improve work procedures.

3. *As the Charge Nurse for a particular ward you are aware that you have very little information about the work that the nurses do and what the patients are like. You believe that a patient data sheet completed by the nurses would be extremely useful. You know that staff will be resistant to the idea as they are already very busy and form filling is generally considered a waste of time. How would you go about introducing the patient data sheet?*

    1 – We are going to introduce a patient data sheet, there is no choice or argument about it.

    or

    Forget about it. I will never be able to convince staff of the value of the patient data sheet. Therefore, they will not bother to complete it and I will have wasted my time.

    3 – Develop form in conjunction with one or two staff or have someone else develop it in consultation with staff.

    or

    Introduce patient data sheet with discussion and participation of staff, trial it, ask for feedback.

    5 – Look at existing data collection. Need to be sure that a new form will save time and/or provide necessary information and gain quality outcomes. Ensure own understanding of the requirements and justifications for introducing a new data collection process. Propose the idea to management. Explain objectives and justification to staff. Enlist their assistance to develop an appropriate form. Explain that it could improve

their situation by showing whether or not they are under resourced. Trial form, seek staff feedback, and modify as required. Introduce finalized form (if successful) as a requirement.

(Note: This question is also strongly related to the competency of people management.)

4. *You have received a request to accommodate overflow patients, on an ongoing basis, from a medical consultant that specializes in a different service area from your particular ward. How would you respond to this request?*

    1 – Refuse to take them. Staff in this ward are not familiar with this service area, it is unreasonable to expect them to cope with a different specialty.

    or

    Accept the request. The staff will just have to learn to cope.

    3 – Tell the consultant that I will consider the request on a case-by-case basis and accept them when possible.

    or

    Accept the request. Ask the consultant if there is anything special that we should know. Ask consultant to provide some in-service training for ward staff.

    5 – View as an opportunity to expand horizons. Meet with the consultant to explore the issues e.g., patient volumes, type of patient care required, length of stay. Find out: what special needs the patients have, what special equipment is necessary, how available is the consultant and house surgeon for the specialty. Evaluate fit with existing patient load. Discuss with staff and management. Define parameters for acceptance/rejection. Ongoing training may be necessary for the particular specialty, perhaps the consultant could run in-service training with the staff and/or develop an information booklet for staff. Implement.

Patient care: Ensures patient safety and provision of high quality patient care, shows concern for the patient and their family, and provides help and support for them and any decisions that they make.

5. *A diabetic patient, well known to yourself and ward staff, is diagnosed as having a brain tumour. Prognosis is poor and doctors are*

keen to treat the patient with radiotherapy. The patient vehemently rejects radiotherapy, stating that she wishes to 'die with dignity'. What would you do in these circumstances?

1 – The doctors must have a good reason to suggest this treatment. The patient should accept their advice in this situation. A little time is better than none.

3 – Discuss the situation with the patient. Find out why she is against radiotherapy. Suggest that she maybe needs more time to think it through more clearly before making up her mind.

or

Support patient and advocate for the patient if her wishes are not being met.

5 – Discuss issues fully with patient, look at other support options (e.g., hospice, home care). Discuss with the doctors what they believe the benefits of radiotherapy would be in this case. Encourage the doctor to discuss the issues more fully with the patient. Support the patient in her decision to reject radiotherapy, if that is what she really wants. Advocate for patient if her wishes are not being met. Endeavour to provide the optimum care for the patient until she dies. Assist medical staff to come to terms with the inevitable death of the patient.

6. *A patient has been receiving regular pethidine throughout his admission. Some of your staff believe his complaints of pain are not genuine. It is three hours since he last had pethidine and he is complaining of severe pain. He is charted pethidine Q4h prn. What would you do?*

1 – I would be concerned that he was potentially or actually a drug abuser and would therefore have the narcotic discontinued.

or

Nothing. Ignore staff comments and continue pain relief four-hourly.

3 – If patients say they have pain, then they have pain. Patients should be listened to. However, pain cannot always be completely eliminated. Investigate the problem with the patient and have his pain relief reviewed as soon as possible.

or

Have patient checked by medical staff.

5 – Any complaint of pain must be taken seriously. Call for a doctor (an acute pain specialist if available) to have the immediate pain problem alleviated. Initiate a thorough nursing and medical reassessment to identify the cause of the continuing complaint. Develop a plan of care to ensure that patient does not experience unnecessary pain. Discuss with staff their concerns. Assess the need for pain management inservice training for staff.

Open communication: Develops and maintains open communication channels with all staff. Distributes and interprets (when necessary) information from, and decisions by, senior management.

7. *It is the Charge Nurse's responsibility to pass on information to their staff. Some information comes in the form of written material such as newsletters and memoranda, and some is verbal information from management meetings. How would you go about ensuring that all of your staff are conversant with and understand the disseminated information?*

1 – Decide that there is too much material and select only some items for posting on the notice board.

or

Put the written information in a folder and tell staff it was there and they could read it if they wanted to.

or

Most of that stuff is not all that important. Leave the information in places that staff are likely to see it.

3 – Ensure that regular formal communication opportunities exist e.g., weekly meetings, communication books, checklists on circulated material etc.

5 – You can't make people read or catch up on information. Provide formal opportunities such as weekly meetings, a communication book, and circulated material. Ask staff how they would like information to be disseminated to them. Communication is more than formal communication, ensure regular opportunity for informal discussion of significant issues. Provide informal opportunities such as raising issues/topics, presenting written information at changeover time, highlight meetings and send staff representatives who can then feedback to the group. Ask staff whenever possible

'Did you see that notice/memo/article on . . .?' Be available to discuss important information that clearly impacts on staff.

8. *Following the recommendation of a consultancy firm, management insisted that all nursing staff in a particular ward complete daily schedules. These schedules were to show the nurses' patients for the day, treatments required and their nursing plan. Staff felt that none of the schedules provided by the consultancy firm were suitable. The nursing staff claimed that they could design a simpler and better schedule. As Charge Nurse of this ward what would your reaction be?*

1 – These forms have been developed by expensive consultants and approved by management. They must be used.

or

Tell staff not to bother completing the form any more. After all, nurses should be spending their time looking after patients, not filling in useless forms.

3 – Listen to staff. Persuade staff to complete the schedules for a specified trial period saying that at the end of this period we will evaluate the success of the new schedules.

5 – Listen to the staff. Ask for their design. Develop it with them. Arrange a meeting with representatives of the consultancy firm and management to discuss the nurses' claims. Advocate the nurses' point of view to management. Suggest to management that resistance to the form could be overcome if the nurses were given the opportunity to design the form themselves. Naturally, the new version would still have to collect all the necessary information.

Staff selection and development: Assesses technical and interpersonal fit of applicants in selection interviews, facilitates the integration of new staff, and shows commitment to employee development.

9. *A couple of incidents in your ward lead you to believe that members of your staff do not have adequate knowledge of a recently introduced procedure. What would you do?*

1 – Put up a notice saying that I am very disappointed with the poor performance of staff in failing to follow correctly a newly introduced procedure. Improvement is expected.

or

Nurses are professionally accountable for their practice. It is their individual responsibility to make sure that they keep up to date with new procedures. Suggest this to the nurses concerned.

3 – Speak to the nurses concerned. Repeat the implementation in-service used when the procedure was first introduced, emphasizing the areas of knowledge shown to be deficient.

or

Carry out an audit of the procedure and point out to staff the problems that have been arising.

5 – Investigate incidents further to clarify cause (i.e., audit procedure). If knowledge deficit is shown to be the problem, identify extent of the deficit among staff. Review procedure to see that it is appropriate. Speak to staff, seek their opinions about the new procedure and ways of ensuring that it is completed properly. Design or have designed an in-service session, or other appropriate form of training, to correct knowledge deficit. Evaluate training and monitor compliance with procedure.

10. *New staff nurses have just been appointed to your ward, and begin today. How would you assist their orientation?*

1 – Assign them a relatively light workload for the duty and see how they manage.

or

Show them around the ward, and then let them go to it.

3 – Welcome them to the ward, assign a senior nurse to act as their 'buddy'. This person should be available to work with, and help orientate, the new member each day for a week. Evaluate progress after one week and decide whether they are ready for autonomous practice.

5 – Make sure that all staff know when the new members are commencing. Welcome each new member and introduce them to staff. Spend an hour with them to establish their level of competency, background and experience and to design a specific plan for their orientation. Introduce them to the ward preceptor who will be responsible for further refining the plan and working with the new staff members over the next few weeks. Ensure that new staff have been booked into any planned orientation days. Evaluate progress each day and after one to four weeks.

Planning: Establishes courses of action to accomplish goals, including establishing time-frames and allocating resources. Demonstrates fairness in designing rosters, makes assessments of workloads and allocates staff accordingly.

11. *As the Charge Nurse you are required to prepare a roster for the ward. How would you go about this? What factors do you consider important?*

> 1 – I would take the existing roster and repeat it. Nursing is a 24hr, seven day-a-week job. Staff have to accept that.
>
> **or**
>
> Rostering is easy. Let the staff do it themselves. They will usually sort things out pretty well.

> 3 – Delegate rostering to one of the staff nurses who has shown an aptitude in this area. Important factors are ensuring right staffing levels at all time, and fairness to all staff.
>
> **or**
>
> Allow staff to roster themselves. Check the roster ensuring that holidays and sick leave have been adequately considered and prepared for.
>
> **or**
>
> Carry out roster according to the needs of the ward and the legal requirements of rostering.

> 5 – Establish seniority and experience of staff, clarify busy and quiet times, determine necessary mix of senior and junior staff, and accommodate staff requests where possible. Important factors are: 1) skill mix; 2) staffing levels; 3) workloads; 4) fairness; 5) interpersonal issues; 6) efficient staff utilization; 7) health issues; and 8) legal requirement of rostering. Design the roster with all of these factors in mind.

12. *It is Monday and it is clearly going to be a very busy week. Besides all the normal daily and weekly activities, you have a new staff nurse starting in your ward tomorrow. You have also been requested by management to prepare a report in support of your request for additional resources for the ward. It is essential that you complete the report by the end of the week, before the resource allocation process begins next Monday. How do you go about ensuring that all of your responsibilities are met on time?*

> 1 – I'm well organized and I can fit everything in as it comes.
>
> **or**

Try to get the report done. However, if it was a day or two late it wouldn't matter too much as it will take longer than a day or two for the resource allocation procedure to finish.

or

Either do the management report or take care of the new staff nurse. There will not be enough time to do them both.

3 – I would make sure I was prepared for the new staff member. Try and complete the report between interruptions. Perhaps, spend extra time at home after work completing the report.

or

Set aside time to write the report by delegating some of my usual duties to other staff members.

5 – Prioritize my commitments for the week. Determine which ones I can delegate to other suitable staff (e.g., normal Charge Nurse duties, preceptor to orientate new staff member). Work out an action plan and schedule for my remaining activities – particularly writing the report and organizing and monitoring the new staff members orientation. Try to write report as early as possible in the week, if necessary remove myself from the ward in order to complete. Ensure that new staff member is welcomed and begins his/her orientation with the ward preceptor.

GLOSSARY

BDI See behavioural description interview.

Behavioural description interview A type of structured interview in which job candidates are asked to describe particular past situations and how they have responded to them.

Critical incident technique A means of conducting a job analysis, often used in developing structured interviews. Subject matter experts (e.g., supervisors, job incumbents) are asked to describe incidents where job incumbents have performed particularly effectively and ineffectively.

Competency A cluster of similar knowledge, skills, abilities or other attributes (KSAOs) necessary to successfully perform a job.

EEO Equal employment opportunities.

Incumbent A person who holds a particular position.

Job analysis A systematic means of collecting job-related information. When used for personnel selection, the principal output of a job analysis is a list of competencies necessary to perform the job successfully.

KSAOs Knowledge, skills, abilities, and other attributes required to successfully perform a job.

Panel interview Two or more interviewers in the same interview.

Performance dimension See competency.

Position A set of duties and accountabilities performed by one individual within the organization (e.g., a position title may be 'Maintenance Engineer, Generation Station 3'). A *position* differs from a *job*, in that only one person can hold a particular position, while in large organizations there are often a number of positions for a particular job (e.g., a job title may be 'Maintenance Engineer', held by five people in five separate generating stations).

Situational interview A type of structured interview in which job candidates are asked how they would respond in hypothetical job situations.

SMEs See subject-matter experts.

Subject-matter expert People consulted during a job analysis who have information about the target job, usually past or present job incumbents and position superiors.

Validity coefficient A number ranging from 0 to 1.0 which represents the degree of relationship between job candidates' scores on a selection method (e.g., ratings after a structured interview) and a measure of their job performance (e.g., performance appraisal ratings).

BIBLIOGRAPHY

The readings listed below can be consulted for further information on structured interviews. See also the lists of references.

Structured interviews in general

Boxall, P. (1990). 'Interviews: The Steps to Success', *Management (New Zealand)*, September, 54–65.

Campion, M.A., Pursell, E.D. and Brown, B.K. (1988). 'Structured Interviewing: Raising the Psychometric Properties of the Employment Interview', *Personnel Psychology*, **41**, 25–42.

Daniel, C. and Valencia, S. (1991), 'Structured Interviewing Simplified', *Public Personnel Management*, **20** (2), 127–34.

Heneman, H.G. III and Schwab, D. (1975), 'Interviewer Validity as a Function of Interview Structure, Biographical Data, and Interviewee Order', *Journal of Applied Psychology*, **60**, 748–53.

Mayfield, E.C. (1964), 'The Selection Interview: A Re-evaluation of Published Research', *Personnel Psychology*, **17**, 239–60.

Motowidlo, S.J., Carter, G.W., Dunnette, M.D., Tippins, N., Werner, S., Burnett, J.R. and Vaughan, M.J. (1992), 'Studies of the Structured Behavioural Interview', *Journal of Applied Psychology*, **77**, 571–87.

Pursell, E.D., Campion, M.A. and Gaylord, S.R. 1980. 'Structured Interviewing: Avoiding Selection Problems', *Personnel Journal*, November, 907–12.

Schwab, D.P. and Henemann, H.G. III. (1969), 'Relationship Between Interview Structure and Interviewer Reliability in an Employment Situation', *Journal of Applied Psychology*, **53**, 214–17.

Searcy, C.A., Woods, P.N., Gatewood, R. and Lance, C. (1993), 'The

Validity of Structured Interviews: A Meta-Analytical Search for Moderators', paper presented at the Society for Industrial & Organizational Psychologists 1993 Annual Meeting, San Francisco, CA.

Wiesner, W.H. and Cronshaw, S.F. (1988), 'A Meta-Analytic Investigation of the Impact of Interview Format and Degree of Structure on the Validity of the Employment Interview', *Journal of Occupational Psychology*, **61**, 275–90.

Wright, P.M., Lichtenfels, P.A. and Pursell, E.D. (1989), 'The Structured Interview: Additional Studies and a Meta-Analysis', *Journal of Occupational Psychology*, **62**, 191–99.

Patterned behavioural description interviews (PBDIs)

Janz, T. (1982), 'Initial Comparisons of Patterned Behaviour Description Interviews Versus Unstructured Interviews', *Journal of Applied Psychology*, **67**, 577–80.

Janz, T. (1986), *Behavioral Description Interviewing*. Boston: Allyn & Bacon.

Janz, T. (1989), 'The Patterned Behavior Description Interview: The Best Prophet of the Future is the Past', in R.W. Eder and G.R. Ferris (eds), *The Employment Interview*, 158–68, Newbury Park, CA: Sage.

Situational interviews

Latham, G.P. (1989), 'The Reliability, Validity and Practicality of the Situational Interview', in R.W. Eder and G.R. Ferris (eds), *The Employment Interview*, 169–82, Newbury Park, CA: Sage.

Latham, G.P., Saari, L.M., Pursell, E.D. and Campion, M.A. (1980), 'The Situational Interview', *Journal of Applied Psychology*, **65**, 422–27.

Latham, G.P. and Saari, L.M. (1984), 'Do People Do What They Say? Further Studies on the Situational Interview', *Journal of Applied Psychology*, **69**, 569–73.

Maurer, S.D. and Fay, C. (1988), 'Effect of Situational Interviews, Conventional Structured Interviews, and Training on Interview Rating Agreement: An Experimental Analysis', *Personnel Psychology*, **41**, 329–44.

Motowidlo, S.J., Dunnette, M.D. and Carter, G.W. (1990), 'An Alternative Selection Procedure: The Low-Fidelity Simulation', *Journal of Applied Psychology*, **75**, 640–47.

Robertson, I., Gratton, L. and Rout, U. (1990), 'The Validity of Situational Interviews for Administrative Jobs', *Journal of Organizational Behavior*, **11**, 69–76.

Stohr-Gilmore, M.K., Stohr-Gilmore, M.W. and Kistler, N. (1990), 'Improving Selection Outcomes With the Use of Situational Interviews:

Empirical Evidence From a Study of Correctional Officers for New Generation Jails', *Review of Public Personnel Administration*, **10** (2), 1–18.

Weekly, J.A. and Gier, J.A. (1987), 'Reliability and Validity of the Situational Interview for a Sales Position', *Journal of Applied Psychology*, **72**, 484–87.

SUBJECT INDEX

AUTHOR INDEX

Human Capability
A Study of Individual Potential and its Application

Elliott Jaques and Kathryn Cason

A major breakthrough in understanding human capability, intelligence, and development theory is reported with the results of Cason/Jaques' conclusive 3-year study. Their field work demonstrates with high reliability and validity that when heavily engrossed in work, individuals process information in four and only four ways which recur in a series of higher orders of information complexity. Further, this hierarchy of mental processing methods corresponds with levels of individual capability and is congruent with levels of work complexity, explaining, at last, the very nature of managerial systems.

This book also presents support for the concurrent theory, first formulated by Dr Jaques in 1956, that individuals mature in capability within predictable patterns, a maturation process that continues throughout life. The authors demonstrate the nature of this maturation beyond adolescence and into old age, and discuss how this view compares with that of Piaget and of IQ studies which posit that capability and intelligence are fully mature by late adolescence. The ability to plot and predict the growth of human potential capability throughout life will alter dramatically our present conceptions in developmental psychology. The social consequences of this work are likely to be substantial and extensive and are addressed by the authors.

An important outcome of this study is the further development of managerial procedures that enable companies to match people with roles, and to develop programs that effectively meet the organization's future human resource requirements.

1994   181 pages   0 566 07652 7

Gower

The Practice of Empowerment
Making the Most of Human Competence

Dennis C Kinlaw

Organizations are downsizing, re-engineering and restructuring at an ever-increasing rate. The challenge now is to find better and better ways of harnessing the mental resources of the people who remain.

Dr Kinlaw, one of America's leading authorities on management development, sees empowerment as a way of improving organizational performance by making the most competent people the most influential most of the time, and his book provides a comprehensive and detailed model for achieving this objective. Drawing on examples and case studies from successful companies, Dr Kinlaw describes a practical, step-by-step process for introducing or extending empowerment in an organization or any part of an organization, and shows how to use feedback, team development and learning to good effect.

For managers considering, or involved in, empowerment programmes, and for concerned HR and training professionals, this new book represents an important resource for improving organizational performance.

Contents

Preface • Introduction • What empowerment is not • The empowerment process • Managing the empowerment process • The meaning of empowerment • The payoffs of empowerment • Targets for empowerment • Strategies for empowerment • Controls for empowerment • New roles and functions • Putting it all together • References • Index.

1995   208 pages   0 566 07570 9

Gower

Teambuilding Strategy

Mike Woodcock and Dave Francis

There is no doubt that working through teams can be an effective way to accomplish tasks in an organization. As Woodcock and Francis point out, though, it is by no means the only one. Managers concerned with human resource strategy cannot afford to assume that teamwork will always be the best option. A number of questions need to be asked before any decision is made, such as:

- what should be the focus of our organization development interventions?
- should we undertake teambuilding initiatives?
- how extensive should the teambuilding initiative be?
- what resources will we need to support our teambuilding initiative?

This book provides a framework within which these questions may be addressed. It presents a structured approach to analysing the key issues, including a series of questionnaires and activities designed to guide the reader through the key strategic decisions that must be taken by any organization contemplating a teambuilding programme. The authors, two of the best known specialists in the field, examine the benefits and dangers of teambuilding as an organization development strategy and offer detailed guidance on further information and resources.

This is the second and considerably reworked edition of *Organisation Development Through Teambuilding*, first published in 1982.

1994   160 pages   0 566 07496 6

Gower